A Critical Analysis of Race, Policy, and Policing

Bassim Hamadeh, CEO and Publisher
John Remington, Executive Editor
Gem Rabanera, Project Editor
Alia Bales, Production Editor
Emely Villacencio, Senior Graphic Designer
Trey Soto, Licensing Coordinator
Natalie Piccotti, Director of Marketing
Kassie Graves, Vice President of Editorial
Jamie Giganti, Director of Academic Publishing

Cover image copyright © 2013 iStockphoto LP/MCCAIG.

Printed in the United States of America.

ISBN: 978-1-5165-3665-8 (pbk) / 978-1-5165-3666-5 (br)

First Edition

A Critical Analysis of Race, Policy, and Policing

Edited by Sean Wilson and Heather Alaniz

Texas Southern University

CONTENTS

INTRODUCTION

Persons of color have been subject to increased levels of surveillance and suspicion by law enforcement agencies historically and contemporarily throughout the United States (Rios, 2011; Duran, 2013; Alexander, 2012). Many crime control policies enforced by law enforcement agencies throughout the United States have targeted communities of color. During the 1970's, President Nixon spearheaded the tough on crime movement that transformed the focus of the criminal justice system from a system focused on offenders (Hagan, 2010). Tough on crime and zero tolerance policies were passed by states and the rehabilitating offenders to a system mostly concerned with punishing and controlling federal government, and the prison population expanded exponentially. A disproportionate amount of the prison population consists of persons of color (Mauer, 2006; Tonry, 2012). Communities of color were impacted by tough on crime policies more than other communities, as incarceration has destroyed many families in communities of color throughout the United States by removing family members from the community for long periods of time (Clear, 2007; Middlemass, 2017). This removal of often young community members has resulted in the disruption of the family, poverty, and high crime rates in communities of color, as formerly incarcerated persons often recidivate after incarceration because they often lack resources and opportunities to better their lives.

Communities of color are also subject to increased levels of social control by law enforcement agencies because these communities are often seen as being communities that need order to control crime (Jones-Brown, 2007; Russell-Browne, 2008). Persons of color are often stereotyped as criminals. Thus, policies and procedures that subject communities of color to increased levels of police surveillance are often seen as necessary to control crime in communities of color. In New York City, unconstitutional policies such as stop-and-frisk, have subjected millions of Black and Latino males to excessive stops and searches. Many of these stops and searches did not yield drugs or contraband (Jones-Brown, Gill, & Trone, 2010). Stop-and-frisk has been a policing policy adopted by law enforcement agencies throughout the United States. A federal court ruled that the manner in which stop-and-frisk was carried out in New York City was unconstitutional; however, policies such as gang ordinances have labeled entire communities as gang members and criminal associates and have subjected communities of color to increased levels of criminal justice system involvement. In the present, communities of color across the United States have become concerned with excessive force used by police, as many unarmed men, women, and children of color have been killed by police officers. These killings of persons of color have resulted in the Black Lives Matter movement, the Say Her Name movement, and other social activist organizations, which have raised awareness about police brutality by engaging in social activism to change flawed criminal justice policies and procedures that negatively impact communities of color.

Since slavery, Black people have had a complicated relationship with the criminal justice system. Many policies have been passed to control the movement and behavior of Blacks in the United States. The first organized forms of policing in America were slave patrollers. Slave patrols were mostly concerned with returning freed slaves to bondage (Gabbidon & Greene, 2018). Jim Crow laws controlled the behavior and movement of Blacks, and during the 1960s, law enforcement officers were often used as tools to suppress constitutionally-protected demonstrations and protests by Blacks that challenged white supremacy in society (Rahtz, 2016). History and research help highlight the complicated relationship that Blacks have had with law enforcement agencies throughout the United States. Section one of this book seeks to analyze the historical and contemporary relationship between Black communities and law enforcement agencies.

Latinos have also had a problematic history with the criminal justice system in America. Policies like SB-1070 in Arizona and stop-and-frisk in New York City and other cities throughout the United States have subjected Latinos to unconstitutional policing practices. Several scholars have highlighted the abusive and dehumanizing nature of policing that is provided to Latino communities (Rios, 2011; Duran, 2013; Martinez, 2016). With the election of President Donald Trump, anti-Black, Latino, and immigrant sentiment has become more mainstream in American society. According to a report by the Southern Poverty Law Center, hate crimes have increased substantially since Trump's election (SPLC, 2018). Trump's Attorney General Jeff Sessions, has embraced an anti-Latino and immigrant ideology that focuses on detaining and deporting undocumented immigrants. Anti-immigrant sentiment does not only impact undocumented immigrants, but also American-born Latinos. Many American-born Latinos were subjected to unconstitutional police stops and searches by law enforcement agencies in Arizona when SB-1070 was enforced (Selden, Pace, & Nunn-Gillman, 2011). Section two of this text seeks to highlight the lived experiences of Latinos who have been subjected to racial profiling and police abuse in the United States.

This book seeks to examine research addressing racial profiling, punitive justice policies, and the use of excessive force by police. Research that examines the oppressive nature of the criminal justice system is often placed in the margins of academia. Thus, this book seeks to highlight critical research on race and ethnicity by bringing it to the forefront. Books like this one seek to expose students to contemporary justice issues by focusing on the lived experiences of communities most impacted by flawed criminal justice policies. It is imperative to highlight research that focuses on the lived experiences of individuals who are targeted for surveillance by the carceral state, because their experiences can help highlight the unconstitutional and inhumane nature of flawed and biased criminal justice policies and promote constitutional justice policies that can improve the lives of people from communities of color. Tough on crime policies have real societal implications that often impact the most powerless segments of society. The editors hope that readers of this anthology will be inspired to challenge unjust criminal justice policies in society.

REFERENCES

Alexander, M. (2012). *The New Jim Crow: Mass incarceration in the age of colorblindness.* New York, NY: The New Press.

Center, S. P. (2018). *The Year in Hate and Extremism.* Montgomery, AL: Southern Poverty Law Center.

Clear, T. (2007). *Imprisoning Communities: How Mass Incarceration Makes Disadvantaged Neighborhoods Worse.* New York, NY: Oxford University Press.

David A. Selden, J. A.-G. (2011). Placing S.B. 1070 And Racial Profiling Into Context, And What S.B. 1070 Reveals About The Legislative Process In Arizona. *Arizona State Law Journal, 43,* 523–1367.

Delores Jones-Brown, J. G. (2010). *Stop, Question & Frisk Policing Practices in New York City: A Primer.* New York, NY: Center on Race, Crime and Justice John Jay College of Criminal Justice.

Duran, R. J. (2013). *Gang life in two cities: An insider's journey.* New York, NY: Columbia University Press.

Hagan, J. (2012). *Who are the Criminals? The politics of crime policy from the age of Roosevelt to the age of Reagan.* Princeton, NJ: Princeton University Press.

Jones-Brown, D. (2007). Forever the symbolic assailant: the more things change, the more they remain the same: *Criminology & Public Policy, 6*(1), 103–121.

Martinez, C. G. (2016). *The neighborhood has its own rules: Latinos and African Americans in South*

Los Angeles. New York, NY: New York University Press.

Mauer, M. (2006). *Race to incarcerate* . New York, NY: New Press.

Middlemas, K. (2018). *Convicted and Condemned: the politics of Prisoner reentry* New York, NY: New York University Press.

Rahtz, H. (2016). *Race, Riots, and the Police*. Boulder, London: Lynne Rienner Publishers Inc.

Rios, V. (2011). *Punished: policing the lives of Black and Latino boys*. New York, NY: New York University Press.

Russell-Brown, K. (2009). *The Color of Crime*. New York, NY: New York University Press.

Shaun Gabbidon, H. T. (2018). *Race and Crime* . Thousand Oaks, CA: Sage Publications Inc.

Tonry, M. (2012). *Punishing Race: A continuing American dilemma*. New York, NY: Oxford University Press.

Weitzer, R., & Tuch, S. A. (2004). Race and Perceptions of Police Misconduct. *Social Problems*, 51(3), 305–325.

PART I

Policing Blacks

African Americans and Racial Profiling by U.S. Law Enforcement

An Analysis of Police Traffic Stops and Searches of Motorists in Nebraska, 2002–2007

Ngozi Caleb Kamalu

Introduction

Empirical research to date suggests significant practice of racial profiling in law enforcement. This research presents the picture of Nebraska's traffic data for any indications of disparate treatment of minorities, between 2002 and 2007. The study also provides valuable insight into the way traffic stops are conducted in our nation's cities and states, as well as helps provide answers regarding the extent/scope, intent and rationale of racial profiling.

This research involves extensive literature review, whose undercurrent assumptions will be tested, using the Nebraska traffic data as a case-study. The main objectives of this study are:

- To establish a nexus between race and bias policing

- To establish the central and emergent theme from numerous empirical researches on the relationship between race and racial profiling as expressed in police stops, searches and arrest.
- To explore the nature, breadth/scope and patterns of exposure of Black motorists and other ethnic minorities to racial profiling.
- To discuss the history of racial profiling
- To analyze the courts' positions on the topic;
- To define racial profiling
- To review related literature on the theme
- To analyze Nebraska's law enforcement data between 2002 and 2007
- To make recommendations regarding policies in order to reduce risks based on bias in law and law enforcement.

This study relies on data from reports submitted to the legislature of the State of Nebraska, from 2002 to 2007. The submissions reflect the information on the aggregate data collected and submitted by the state of Nebraska's law enforcement establishment covering this period. The data formed the basis of the traffic stops in Nebraska, submitted under the auspices of the Nebraska Commission on Law and Criminal Justice of April 1, 2008.

As a matter of impact, the researcher believes that his findings will assist the law enforcement community, government and stake holders in the criminal justice sectors in the following manner:

- To reduce biased law enforcement which swells the prison population and negatively affects productivity, family life and strains national, state and local financial resources.
- Devise ways to diffuse the tension between law enforcement and the minority community
- Renew the diminishing legitimacy of the government on the part of its ethnic minorities who perceive its actions as mostly unjust, illegal and unequal, degrading, humiliating and racist.

In conclusion, the study presents the "good practices" in policing as supported by academic research. It also examines the merits and shortcomings of racial profiling on effective law enforcement policing and ends by recommending necessary and effective reforms that would enhance the image and tactics of law enforcement before the public. By so doing, the appropriateness of policing practices would become more acceptable to both the police and the general public; and legitimizing them as effective law enforcement strategies in the promotion of good police-community relations worthy of serving as a model of police practices in the State of Nebraska in particular and the United States at large.

In this study, the terms "black" and "African American" will be used synonymously. Also, "racial profiling" will be used interchangeably with "bias" policing.

Ethnic Profiling: Concept and Definitions

Definition1.: Racial profiling is defined by Barlow, David E. and Barlow, Hickman M (2002) as "any situation in which race is used by a police officer or agency to determine the potential criminality of an individual" _Definition 2_: In the words of Goodey, Joe (2006), "The police practice of stopping someone for questioning or searching on the basis of their ethnic or racial appearance and not because of their behavior or because they match an individual suspect description." Goodey argued that ethnic profiling practices in America and abroad have been given impetus by the terrorist attacks in 2001. He argues that law enforcement agencies have expanded it to target Muslim and Arab communities; and that the negative stereotyping of target groups has served to support and reinforce the practice of ethnic profiling. He observed that over representation of minority populations in arrest and prison figures has only served to justify the over-policing of minority groups. He further argued that crimes of the streets (petit/minor misdemeanors), rather than crimes of the suites ("white collar") continue to occupy the minds of the public, media and politicians. As such he concluded that minority communities find themselves on the receiving end (victims) of police attention that is compounded or made worse by the real and perceived threats that flow out of ethnic profiling practices by law enforcement agencies.

History, Evolution and Dynamics of Racial Profiling

The phrase "racial profiling" has been primarily used to denote police bias and stereotypes in its law enforcement practices on the basis of racial and ethnic consideration. For the purpose of this study, racial profiling is the disparate and disproportionate targeting of racial minorities for traffic stops, searches, arrests, detention, and charges. These pretext stops, according to the line police law enforcement officers, offer them the opportunity to stop, detain and in some cases search drivers that the police officers believe or suspect may be involved in other criminal activities, such as weapons and illegal immigrant smuggling as well as drug trafficking. The history of racial profiling has it root in the "war on drugs" which is perceived to have minorities as its primary target. The widespread use of cocaine in the 1980s and the stereotypical association of minorities as the primary users of cocaine by the majority population driven by negative popular media coverage of the issue reinforced the notion that Black and Hispanic minorities, especially males are criminals. This perception which later permeated law enforcement made them prime targets of police stops, search and arrest in many communities.

As the police made more arrests, the courts became overwhelmed and the prison population swelled to the extent that the United States is now designated as the most incarcerated nation in the world. Further, in 1986, the drug Enforcement Agency (DEA) introduced a racially biased drug courier profile designed as a drug-fighting template in its war on drugs program dubbed "operation Pipeline". According to Harris (1999), The DEA relied too much on pretext in its law enforcement. The means of law enforcement involves using minor traffic infraction, whether real or imagined, as an excuse to stop and search vehicles and its passengers. In fact, in the U.S. Supreme Court validated and upheld the use of pretext in traffic law enforcement in Whren V. U.SA (1996).

Having internalized the notion that use of drugs is cultural and that most drug offenses are committed by minorities, law enforcement officials believed that profiling, searching, arresting, prosecuting and imprisoning black and Hispanic youth are the most effective ways of fighting drugs. Hence, the declaration of war on minorities by law-enforcement establishments was justified. As police target minorities for drug search, the more they find drugs, as well as other contrabands such as firearms in a disproportionate number. As a consequence, more minority persons are arrested, prosecuted, jailed or convicted. In an economy with high unemployed youth and lack of skills among them, a revolving door system is established as more minorities came under the domain of law enforcement agencies in one way or another—awaiting trial, under plea-bargain negotiation, under probation or in prison. This cycle eventually reinforced the narrative that criminal activity falls under the domain of minorities and that the only way to stamp out crime is to focus police activity on black and Hispanic youths. Eventually, the direct societal connection of drugs with minorities became a self-fulfilling prophecy.

Many studies, however, have shown that innocent motorists have become victims of such law enforcement practices, especially during the stops, some of which have possibly led to police searches for drugs and other contraband after the subjects of search have already been informed that they have been stopped otherwise, for other causes and pretentions, such as broken tail light, worn out tires, unclearly displayed tags or other minor traffic violations such as the absence of seatbelts.

The assumption that more minority youth are committing crime gave the police the justification to automatically target them for traffic stop, frisk, search, ticketing and eventually, arrest. In fact, race of the group did not escape this criminal brush as most law enforcement officials equated being "black and "Hispanic" as tantamount to drug use and related criminal activities.

Hence, it is not a surprise when the Mauer, Potler and Wolf of The Sentencing Project (1999) reported that 1.7 million inmates in the United States were under the supervision of the criminal justice system, either awaiting trial or actually incarnated; and that 400,000 of this number were charged for drug offenses. Among this population, the report notes that blacks make up 13% of all drug users; 55% of those convicted; 37% of those under arrest for drug possession, use or sale and 74% of all incarcerated drug offenders.

The Supreme Court's Expansion of Police/Law Enforcement Powers: Implications for Racial Profiling

The Fourth Amendment to the American constitution is the part of the Bill of Rights that guards against an individual's unreasonable search and seizure. Under its interpretation, the amendment requires search and arrest warrants obtained from the courts and supported by probable cause. In other words, the fourth amendment protects persons from being stopped or detained by the government without evidence of involvement in criminal activity.

Under normal circumstances, the fourth amendment shields individuals from falling victim to unfair or pre-textual traffic stops, searches or seizure. A pre-textual traffic stops is one in which the arresting officer uses a minor infraction, such as broken tail light, worn out tire or hanging windshield wiper as a pretext to pull over a vehicular driver/motorist, even though his/her real and actual intent is to stop the driver for an unrelated reason, such the persons race or ethnicity.

Given the fact that probable cause means many things to different people and can be taken advantage of by law enforcement officers to stop, search and arrest whomever they want anywhere, anytime, given the confusing nature of traffic laws and the ambiguities posed by the 'probable cause' doctrine. Notwithstanding the legal outcome of any court challenges, what is clear is that courts blunt interpretation of the fourteenth amendment that has expanded the power of the police and less protective of the rights of individuals. The existence of case laws pertaining to the expansion of police powers poses huge implications for the good of the entire community, public justice and especially racial minorities with respect to racial profiling decisions and enforcement.

Traffic enforcement has posed a major constitutional problem for police departments and other law-enforcement agencies throughout the United States. In some of these cases, the courts were presented with the question of whether or not a vehicle search is constitutional even when the officer faked his real motive and intention of initiating a stop, search and arrest.

As a consequence, a myriad of lawsuits have been filed over the years challenging such biased police practices and their resulting charges and penalties. One of these cases for example, has recognized the right of citizens to a fair apprehension by the police. A case in point is the case of *Mapp V. Ohio* (1961). It was in this case that the Supreme Court adopted the "exclusionary rule", in which illegally seized evidence could not be used in court due to procedural error in evidence gathering, even though it could prove the guilt of the accused. This decision may be interpreted to mean that police could not conduct a search on private property without a court order or warrant. Even in a public place, law enforcement agents could not arrest persons without a warrant, unless they have probable cause, in which the officer believes that a crime has been committed. Even in cases where an arrest without warrant or court permission has been made, police must present the accused before a magistrate to justify whether a probable course even existed to warrant and justify the arrest. Under this rule, Police do not have a broad right to stop and frisk people on the street or in their automobiles to make random checks or searches.

However, other land mark Supreme Court cases appear to give credence to police tactics of racial profiling in community policing. Cases in point are not far-fetched. In *Wolf V. Colorado* (1949), the court ruled that any illegally obtained evidence did not necessarily have to be excluded from trial in all cases. In the case of *Terry V. Ohio* (1968), the Supreme Court established the principle that the Fourth Amendment did not prohibit the police or any other law enforcement agent from stopping a person for questioning as long as they have reasonable suspicion that the target or victim might be armed and therefore pose a danger, even when that suspicion does not equate the probable cause standard necessary for an arrest. Terry would prove to be one of the legal tools used by law enforcement agencies in defense of racial profiling practices.

In *Whren V. United States* (1996), the court was confronted with its first major decision on the constitutionality of police traffic stops based on "virtual pretext". The Supreme Court ruled that the temporary detention of motorists upon probable cause to believe that he has violated traffic laws does not violate the Fourth Amendment prohibition against unreasonable search and seizure, even if a reasonable law enforcement officer would not have stopped the motorist, absent some additional law enforcement objectives. In other words, a police officer who observes a minor traffic violation or offense like broken or burnt out tail light, faulty brake light, cracked windshield, failure to signal when changing lane, driving too close to cars in front, worn out tires, loose seat belt, poor exhaustion emission, absence of headlight under rain, may stop the driver even if a reasonable officer would not have been motivated to stop the car by desire to enforce the traffic laws. The officer may then ask the driver questions unrelated to the purported purpose of the stop, and may attempt to secure consent to search the car.

In *Ohio V. Robinette (1996)*, the court ruled that officers are not required to inform motorists at the end of a traffic stop that they are free to go before seeking permission to search the motorist's car. Put another way, an officer is not obligated to tell a driver that he or she can refuse an officer's request for a search. In *Maryland V. Wilson (1997)*, the court took the position that an officer making a traffic stop may order passengers to get out of the car pending completion of the stop. In other words, the officer is given the sweeping power, authority and discretion to order passengers out of stopped cars, irrespective of whether or not there is a reason or probable cause or an inclination that they are dangerous. In *Wyoming V. Houghton (1999)*, the Supreme Court ruled that police officers with probable cause to search a car may inspect passenger's belongings which are found or located in the car that are capable of concealing the object of the search. Presented another way, Pursuant to the arrest of the driver of a flagged traffic, the police can search items and objects that cannot be clearly seen with a naked eye, such as closed purse of a passenger even without probable cause or a reasonable belief that a person has committed an offense. In the case of *Thornton V. United States (2004)*, the Supreme Court ruled that when a police officer makes a lawful custodial arrest of a vehicular occupant, he/she has the right and discretion to search the automobile passenger's compartment as a contemporaneous incident of arrest. This means that the officer may get into other related or unrelated activities, such as searching for drugs, guns or evidence of a crime while arresting the automobile's drivers or passengers. The reasoning of the court is that all the activities or events listed are extensions of each other, and that since each action happens at the same time as the others, all the issues constitute one continuum.

Racial Profiling Concerns Across the States and the Nation

Public concern over police excesses and conducts regarding racial profiling have grown over the years. As a consequence, Representatives John Conyers (D-Michigan) and Senator Frank Lautenberg (D-New Jersey) introduced bill to congress that would offer incentives for police departments to generate and keep detailed records of traffic stops, including gender, race and ethnicity of the subjects of search, as well as document whether a search was initiated by the officer or/ and if any citations or warnings were issued. A number of states, including North Carolina and Connecticut have enacted legislation mandating states and local law enforcement personnel to collect data on motorists. At the same time, others are considering to pass similar legislations. States such as New Jersey and Maryland have acceded to such requirement of collecting data on motorist stops as a result of consent decrees resulting from cases filed against them by the United States Department of Justice.

Although statistics on racial profiling is both limited and scanty, there appears to be overwhelming evidence to suggest that in certain localities, minority drivers are stopped, interrogated and frisked much more often than white motorists. For example, Harris (1997), based on 1, 100 videotaped traffic stops in a three-year study on I-95 of Volusia County, Florida, found that although minority (African-Americans and Hispanics) make up only about 55% of the motorists on this highway, they comprised more than 70% of the drivers stopped for suspected traffic violations and offenses. Furthermore, despite the fact that out of the 1,100 traffic stops executed, only 9 tickets involving Hispanics or African Americans were issued. On the average also, these minority drivers were detained on the average, two times as long as their white counterparts.

In another look at the State of Maryland, Harris (1997) also found that out of 732 motorists searched by the Maryland State Police between January 1995 and June 1996, 75% of the motor vehicle searches conducted belonged to African American motorists. In another report of traffic study conducted in the city of San Diego between January 2000 and June 2000,

Cordner, William and Zuniga (2000) found that out of 91, 552 traffic stops conducted Hispanics and African Americans were more than their population percentages warranted, in terms of those who were stopped, searched and arrested compared with whites. For example, the researchers found that African Americans aged 15 years or older, who comprised only 20.2% of the San Diego's population, recorded 34.9 % of equipment violation stops and 50.1% of the searches subsequent to vehicular stops. With respect to African Americans, the investigators found that residents aged 15 years and older, who made up 8% of San Diego's population, represented 14.3% of equipment violation stops and 19.5% of searches leading to vehicle stops.

Literature Review on Police Traffic Stops, Searches, Arrests, and Other Enforcements

Hernandez-Murillo and Knowles (2004) observed that state wide reports on police traffic stops and searches summarize large populations and therefore reduce them to powerful tools for identifying racial bias especially when other data, such as search outcomes are included. However, they note that when reported statistics are joined with information on searches involving different levels of police discretion, then standard tests for racial bias tend not to be applicable. While the researchers conclude that their tests reject unbiased policing as an explanation of the disparate impact of motor-vehicle searches on minorities in Missouri, they recommend a model of police search decisions that could allow for nondiscretionary searches as well as come up with tests for racial bias in data that mix different search types.

Greg Ridgeway (2006) acknowledged that in response to community demands, case settlements and state laws affecting racial profiling, police departments all over the United States are compiling data on traffic stops, but, there is no consensus method of analyzing all the data being collated. Rather, he maintains much of the focus has been on benchmarks for the race distribution of stops and searches. While noting that little empirical work has been able to advance our

understanding of the influence of race in the post-stop activities of police, he proposed the *propensity score* technique as an effective and more reliable method to determine the extent to which race-bias affects citation rates, search rates and the duration of traffic stops.

Weitzer and Tuch (2006) noted that even though racial profiling by the police has become an increasing issue of great controversy in the United States, yet little is known about the breadth of the problem and the scope of public perception of the racial profiling phenomenon. On the basis of extensive analysis of recent national survey data on the attitudes of the public on racial profiling, the researchers suggested that both race and personal profiling experience are strong predictors of attitudes toward profiling. They also concluded that among African Americans, social class affected views and attitudes as well as the prevalence of their attitudes and acceptability toward profiling practices. They then suggested that more studies are needed to determine the extent to which class influences enforcement decisions and evaluations by the Police.

Weizer and Tuch (1999), initially operated on the premise of previous research that shows that blacks are more likely than whites to hold unfavorable opinions of the criminal justice agencies, but set to find the level at which social class affects racial profiling opinions. Relying on national survey data on the perceptions of racial discrimination by the Police and the Criminal Justice System, the study set to find the connection between race and class in shaping citizen attitudes toward racial profiling. The findings of the study are aligned with that of 2006, that concluded that both race and class are strong predictors of racial attitudes toward racial profiling, except in the case of its conclusion that middle-class Blacks are sometimes more critical of the police and the justice system and racial profiling system than are lower-class Blacks.

Walker (2008), responding to mounting allegations of racial and ethnic discrimination in traffic stops (Racial profiling) notes that law enforcement agencies are now collecting data on traffic stops that include the racial and ethnic identity of the driver. This method, he argues is replete with all kinds of difficulties because interpreting these complex data on traffic stops that include race and the ethnicity of drivers is very complex. Using the examination of traffic stop data from the San Jose Police Department as a case study, Walker (2008) maintained that although the baselines commonly used, (such as Census data, Observation of roadway usage, Official accident data, Assessment of traffic violation behavior, Citizen surveys, and Internal departmental comparisons) were appropriate while reliance on resident population data and/or official crime data are not adequate as baselines. The study proposed the use of police early warning system as an alternative.

Dunham et al. (2005) examined the formation of police suspicion and the mental processes and decisions made by officers before traffic enforcement—stopping and questioning motorists, including the outcomes of such stops. The authors relied on observational studies of police decision making in Savannah Georgia. In their research design, the researchers put into consideration the major categories of reasons given by officers for becoming suspicious of motorists. In other words the "probable cause" factors likely to spur them into traffic enforcement stop. Among the reasons identified were appearance, information, behavior and time. The findings of the research appeared inconsistent with the study's early assumption and speculation that major

incidents of discrimination take place during the presto (high speed or tempo) stage in the Officer's decision making process. The authors found that several stops and other decisions made by the police were unacceptable, having been based on non-behavioral criteria (targeting). More specifically, the officers did not make some of the decisions in direct natural response or reaction to the conduct of the motorist.

Alpert et al. (2007) argues that minority communities have paid too much attention to concern over the improper use of race by law enforcement officers. Their study was designed to test and investigate the claims that the Miami-Dade Florida Police department uses racial profiling techniques in making traffic stops and conducting post-stop activities, using a complex methodological approach. The study showed mixed results. First, it found that the Officers' aggregate actions do not show any patterns of discrimination toward minority citizens during traffic stop encounters. However, it partially indicated some level of discrimination on the post-stop activities side, where some disparate treatments of minorities in comparison with the majority population were detected.

Nevertheless, the investigators went further in making policy recommendations on how to mitigate the incident of racial profiling in law enforcement. Some of the recommendations put forward include: having clear policies and directives that explain the proper use of race in decision making among police departments; using intelligence tools that rely on suspicion as opposed to the race of the motorist; training law enforcement officers on the consequences of using race as a factor in law enforcement decisions; maintaining a data-collection and analytic system to monitor the activities of officers as it pertains to the race of the motorist; the generation and preservation of a record of police-citizen encounter and interrogation for later intelligence and court processes; and the use of record checks in the field that can trigger a process that results in the detection and arrest of motorists.

Rojek et. al (2004) who detected a few consistent research findings and literature regarding the influence of race and ethnic differences in traffic stops, searches and arrests, set to find answers to the potential bias associated with the use of "baselines", such as residential population data to estimate the racial composition of drivers in a community. Using a special estimation method that computes the racial composition of drivers in a given locality based on the size and composition of nearby areas, and applying it to traffic stop data for 92 Missouri municipalities, the authors were able to produce more accurate estimates for several suburban areas ringing the city of St. Louis than those based on residential population data of racial disparity in traffic stops. The investigators concluded that there was small but persistent group difference in the probability of motorists being pulled over by the police in the 92 communities and a somewhat larger difference in the probability of drivers being searched and arrested.

Petrocelli et. al (2003) conducted a study designed to explore whether police traffic stops, search and arrest practices differed according to racial or socio-economic factors among selected neighborhoods. Using data collected by Richmond Virginia Police Department, and applying the "conflict theory" in their analysis, the researchers drew a number of conclusions among which are: that the total number of stops made by Richmond police were determined solely by the crime rate of the neighborhood; that there was a direct correlation between the percentage of blacks in the community and the percentage of stops that eventually resulted in traffic searches. The conclusions drawn from the study suggested that the percentage of Black population and the area crime rate primarily influenced the percentage of vehicular stops of black motorists ending in arrest/summons.

Brian N. Williams and Michael Stahl (2008) conducted a two-approach study—an analytical study of traffic stop data of two states and twenty four local police agencies during the 2001 calendar year using a focus group interviewing technique of groups of officers from five participating agencies. The objectives of their study were to determine whether race is a significant predictor of positive search results of police officers during traffic stops; whether race was the sole determinant of whom a victim of police search really is; and to determine the perceptions of officers regarding the use of race in community law enforcement decisions. The study concluded that race did correlate with "fruitful" traffic stops.

DATA ANALYSES

Table 1.1.1: The 2007 Annual Report of the Missouri Vehicle Stops issued by the Missouri Attorney General Jay Nixon indicated in the following table showed impressive results. With respect to "*search rate,*" (the % of stops in which a search is conducted), one of the indexes used to measure racial-profiling, the search rate for all motorists was 7.91%. The search rate for white motorists was 6.86; 12.26% for Blacks; 14.96 for

TABLE 1.1.1 Data Presentation: 2007 Annual Report Missouri Vehicle Stops

Key Indicators	Total	White	Black (African American)	Hispanic	Asian
Population	4,632,578	3,888,907	496,788	102,685	69,553
Traffic Stops	1,564,452	1,240,821	264,307	34,609	12,651
Searches	123,808	85,145	32,405	5,179	436
Arrests	89,537	61,004	24,008	3,812	299
State-wide Population %	100%	83.95%	10.72%	2.22%	1.50%
Disparity Index	—	.95	1.58	1.00	.54
Search Rate	7.91%	6.86%	12.26%	14.96%	3.45%
Contraband Hit Rate	21.17%	23.01%	17.60%	14.40%	14.68%
Arrest Rate	5.72%	4.92%	9.08%	11.01%	2.36%

Hispanics, 3.45% for Asians and 10.83% for American Indians. In comparison, the search rate for Hispanic motorists was the highest, followed by those of blacks, American Indians and then Whites, while that of Asians was the least.

With respect to *disparity index*, which is the proportion of stops/proportion of population, the disparity index for Whites is .95, Blacks (1.58), Hispanics (1.00), Asians (.54), and American Indians (.18). This means that Blacks with a disparity index >1 are overrepresented in the search, while the disparity indexes of Whites, Asians, and American Indians, which are < 1 indicate underrepresentation in search rate; while Hispanics with a disparity index of 1.00 indicate no disparity.

In terms of *contraband hit rate* (searches in which contraband are found), of the overall percentage contraband hit rate of 21.17%, the rate for White motorists is 23.01%, Blacks (17.60%), Hispanics (14.40%), Asians (14.68%), and American Indians (24.38%).

With regard to *arrest rate* (Arrests made within the number of traffic stops), of the total arrest rate for all motorists of 5.72%, the White rate was 4.92%, Blacks (9.08%), Hispanics (11.01%, Asians (2.36%) and

American Indians (7.37%). The data here also suggest that the probability/chances of arrest vary across ethnic and racial groups.

Table 1.1.2: Analysis shows that the total traffic stops reported between 2002 and 2007 was highest among whites (86%) followed by distant second, Hispanics (6.7%) and a distant Third, Blacks (4.9%). All other racial categories, Asian Pacific Islander (0.9%), Native America/Alaskan (0.8%) were stopped throughout this period at a total rate of less than 1%.

Table 1.1.3: With respect to data, the reasons for traffic stop show that the officers were presented with numerous options on which to charge potential violators, including traffic code violation (speeding, expired license plate, worn out tires, broken tail lights and exhaust smoke etc.). The officer could also initiate a traffic stop on the basis of criminal code violation, such as driving a stolen vehicle, having a standing court warrant, driving without license, driving with expired license, unpaid ticket, and carrying contraband—drugs and/or firearm. These violations would fetch a motorist custodial arrest. From 2002 and 2007, the overwhelming majority of all stops (95.1%) were for traffic code violation. However, there was

TABLE 1.1.2 **Traffic Stops Reported in Nebraska.**

Racial/ Ethnic Group Category	2002	2003	2004	2005	2006	2007	2002–2007 Total
	# (%)	# (%)	# (%)	# (%)	# (%)	# (%)	# (%)
Asian/Pacific Islander	4,490 (0.8%)	4,484 (0.9%)	4,844 (1.0%)	5,082 (1.0%)	4,790 (1.0%)	4,801 (0.9%)	27,985 (0.9%)
Black (African American)	26,239 (5.0%)	23,331 (4.7%)	23,143 (4.7%)	24,572 (5.0%)	23,530 (5.1%)	23,671 (5.1%)	144,309 (4.9%)
Hispanic	32,241 (6.7%)	34,303 (6.9%)	33,301 (6.8%)	33,371 (6.8%)	30,763 (6.7%)	32,253 (7.0%)	199,891 (6.7%)
Native American/ Alaskan	3,960 (0.7%)	3,651 (0.7%)	3,911 (0.8%)	3,859 (0.8%)	3,906 (0.8%)	3,918 (0.8%)	22,886 (0.8%)
Other	2,951 (0.6%)	2,956 (0.6%)	3,110 (0.6%)	3,688 (0.8%)	4,276 (0.9%)	4,273 (0.9%)	20,855 (0.7%)
White	455,414 (86.2%)	426,615 (86.1%)	420,413 (86.0%)	417,678 (85.5%)	394,589 (85.4%)	394,215 (85.1%)	2,546,359 (86.0%)
TOTAL	528,295 (100%)	495,340 (100%)	488,722 (100%)	488,220 (100%)	461,854 (100%)	463,131 (100%)	2,962,285 (100%)

TABLE 1.1.3 Reason for the Stop in Nebraska—2002–2007.

Racial/ Ethnic Group Category	Traffic Code Violation		Criminal Code Violation		Other		Unknown	
	#	%	#	%	#	%	#	%
Asian/Pacific Islander	27,105	96.9	341	1.2	501	1.8	38	0.1
Black (African American)	136,271	94.4	3,167	2.2	4,839	3.4	32	0.0
Hispanic	187,751	93.9	4,425	2.2	7,492	3.7	224	0.1
Native American/Alaskan	19,806	86.5	811	3.5	2,169	9.5	100	0.4
Other	19,295	92.5	319	1.5	1,152	5.5	89	0.4
White	2,427,703	95.3	31,546	1.2	81,002	3.2	6,108	0.2
TOTAL	2,817,931	95.1	40,609	1.4	97,155	3.3	6,591	0.2

no significant disparity among the various racial/ethnic groups when broken down. Each registered a high percentage score ranging from 86.5% to 96.9%. In terms of criminal code violation, a small or meager total percentage of stops (1.4%) were made under criminal code rationales. Native Americans/Alaskans registered the highest total (3.5%), while Whites and Asian/Pacific Islander recorded the least (1.2%). The total rate of stop among Blacks and Hispanics were equal (2.2%).

Table 1.1.4: The analysis of disposition of the traffic stop outcomes from 2002 to 2007 shows that Black motorists have the highest likelihood (18.7%) to be arrested and detained (*custodial arrest*). A custodian arrest could be triggered not only by a traffic arrest, but by other serious violations and infractions that include—Driving Under Influence/Intoxication, driving without license or with expired one or having a pending court arrest warrant. The Asian/Pacific Islander is the least likely group at (2.6%), followed by Whites (2.9%) to come under custodial arrest. Blacks were arrested at a rate of approximately six times as Whites (18.7% to 2.9%). As regards *ticketing*, Hispanics receive the highest percentage of tickets (40.5%) followed by Asian/Pacific Islander (39.8%) and then Blacks (36.8%). Whites at (34.9%) are prone to receive the least percentage of tickets, next to Blacks (36.8%). With respect to *verbal warning*, Blacks received the most (12%), followed by Hispanics and Asian/Pacific Islander at 12% each. In contrast, Whites received the least (6.9%), followed by Native American/Alaskan (8.3%).

Whites and Asian/Pacific Islander most commonly received written warning (41.6 : 37.4%), followed by Hispanic and Native American/Alaskan groups who received about the same amount of written warnings (28.1% : 28%), and then Blacks at (22.2%).

Table 1.1.5: The examination of data on searches conducted by law enforcement following a traffic stop from 2001 to 2007 reveal that members of Native American/Alaskan, Hispanic and Black groups were more often searched (6.7% : 6.6% : 4.85) than the larger population at the rate of (3.4%).

That means that vehicular stops involving Native Americans/Alaskan, Hispanic and Black groups are more likely to lead to searches being conducted in relation to stops (3.4%) among all drivers. Also, aggregate data from 2002 to 2007 show that stops involving Hispanic (6.6%) and Native American/Alaskan people (6.7%) were almost two times as likely to result in searches compared to the general population (3.4%). On the other hand, stops involving persons of white (3.1%) and Asian/Pacific Islander (2.2%) groups are less likely to degenerate into searches relative to the entire population (3.4%).

TABLE 1.1.4 **Disposition of the Traffic Stop (Outcome) in Nebraska—2002–2007.**

	Custodial Arrest		Ticket		Verbal Warning		Written Warning		Defect Card		No Action		Unknown	
	#	%	#	%	#	%	#	%	#	%	#	%	#	%
Asian/ Pacific Islander	726	2.6	11,148	39.8	2,747	9.8	10,477	37.4	1,965	7.0	807	2.9	115	0.4
Black (African American)	26,955	18.7	53,057	36.8	17,304	12.0	32,035	22.2	7,625	5.3	6,314	4.4	1,019	0.7
Hispanic	16,411	8.2	80,865	40.5	19,682	9.8	56,108	28.1	18,227	9.1	7,260	3.6	1,338	0.7
Native American/ Alaskan	2,150	9.4	8,563	37.4	1,910	8.3	6,417	28.0	2,587	11.3	1,130	4.9	129	0.6
Other	2,458	11.8	7,269	34.9	3,647	17.5	5,376	25.8	566	2.7	1,435	6.9	104	0.5
White	75,078	2.9	887,407	34.9	175,845	6.9	1,058,504	41.6	244,449	9.6	93,869	3.7	11,207	0.4
TOTAL	123,778	4.2	1,048,309	35.4	221,135	7.5	1,169,817	39.5	275,419	9.3	110,825	3.7	13,912	0.5

TABLE 1.1.5 **Searches Conducted as part of a Traffic Stop in Nebraska.**
Percentages are % of race of total stops made.

Racial/Ethnic Group Category	2002	2003	2004	2005	2006	2007	2002–2007 Total
	# (%)	# (%)	# (%)	# (%)	# (%)	# (%)	# (%)
Asian/Pacific Islander	139 (3.1%)	96 (2.1%)	105 (2.2%)	87 (1.7%)	106 (2.2%)	106 (2.2%)	625 (2.2%)
Black (African American)	1,472 (5.6%)	1,079 (4.6%)	1,066 (4.6%)	999 (4.0%)	1,211 (5.1%)	1,211 (5.1%)	6,977 (4.8%)
Hispanic	2,428 (6.9%)	2,351 (6.9%)	2,027 (6.1%)	1,876 (5.6%)	2,151 (6.7%)	21,151 (6.7%)	13,208 (6.6%)
Native American/Alaskan	191 (4.8%)	208 (5.7%)	297 (7.6%)	314 (8.1%)	297 (7.6%)	297 (7.6%)	1,534 (6.7%)
Other	169 (5.7%)	61 (2.1%)	69 (2.2%)	96 (2.2%)	113 (2.6%)	113 (2.6%)	611 (2.9%)
White	14,899 (3.3%)	13,691 (3.2%)	12,981 (3.1%)	12,888 (3.0%)	12,074 (3.0%)	12,074 (3.1%)	78,349 (3.1%)
TOTAL	19,298 (3.7%)	17,486 (3.5%)	16,545 (3.4%)	16,260 (3.3%)	15,952 (3.4%)	15,952 (3.4%)	101,304 (3.4%)

Conclusion and Recommendations

Allegations of racial profiling are hard to prove. This is because of differing perceptions and interpretations of police actions. Individual perceptions of police actions can be construed based on many factors such as cultural factors, environment, physical surrounding, time of day, and danger. Some actions may be interpreted in different ways based on expectations of restraint, courtesy and excessive use of force. Others may be misinterpreted because law enforcement decisions and actions by the police are products of reasonable suspicion' by the police, such as whether reasonable suspicion exists; whether the suspect fits the description of the offender; whether there is an attempt on the part of the suspect to escape; whether the suspect is responsive to the officer's questioning; whether the suspect has prior criminal record; whether the suspect was seen around the crime scene; whether the suspect was supposed to be in the area at the time the crime was committed or reported; and whether the suspects' conducts and behaviors mimic the pattern or modus operandi used by law enforcement.

These factors often drive police responses, rather than actual proof regarding the commission of the crime. Although the courts have grappled with the complexity of the issue, they appear to lean in favor of the law enforcement through their decisions in a series of high-profile cases that include but are not limited to: Mapp V. Ohio (1961); Wolf V. Colorado (1949); Terry V. Ohio (1968); Whren V. United States (1996); Maryland V. Wilson (1997); Wyoming V. Houghton (1999) and Thornton V. United States (2004).

Nevertheless, in order to strike a balance between the law enforcement need to fight crime and protect society, and the right of citizens to reasonable constitutional protection, the following recommendations are being proposed:

- Initiating reforms in police training and policing, such as police-community policing
- Instituting community-police control groups to diffuse conflicts surrounding police brutality, excessive use of force and racial profiling.
- Promote public education on the problem of racial profiling, using seminars and workshops
- Implementing a computerized system of storing and retrieving information on police activities such as audio-visual aids like cameras for permanent record keeping.
- Instituting sensitivity training for inexperienced officers and those whose record show "cause" for concern
- Establishing hotline and toll-free numbers to make it easy for citizens to file or report complaints
- Requiring police agencies and the Attorney Generals' offices to issue periodic/annual reports on the state of policing in the states.
- Making sure that minorities make up "critical mass" of recruits and officers' ranks in order to promote diversity in law enforcement, and boost public ownership and confidence in the police and law enforcement establishments.
- Establishing taskforces and/or citizen review boards to investigate and recommend disciplinary measures and actions against officers implicated in bias-policing.

REFERENCES

Albert, Geoffrey P. et al. (2007). "Investigating Racial Profiling by the Miami-Dade Police Department: A Multi-method Approach," *Criminology and Public Policy*, Vol. 6, No/Issue. 1, March, pp. 25–55.

Barlow, David E. and Barlow, Hickman Melissa (2002). "Racial Profiling: A Survey of African American Police officers," *Police Quarterly*, Vol. 5, No. 3, pp. 334–358.

Cordner, G., Williams, B. & Zuniga, M. (2000). Vehicle Stop study mid-year Report. San Diego Police Department, San Diego, California.

Dunham, Roger G. (2005) "Transforming citizens into suspects: Factors that Influence the Formation of Police Suspicion," *Police Quarterly*, Vol. 8, No. 3, pp. 366–393.

Goodey, Jo (2006). "Ethnic Profiling, Criminal (In) Justice and Minority Populations." *Critical Criminology*, Volume 14, pp. 207–212.

Harris, David. A. (1997). Driving while black and all other traffic offenses: The Supreme Court and pretext traffic stops. *The Journal of Criminal law and Criminology*, 87, 544–582.

Harris, David A. (1997). "Driving While Black: Racial Profiling on Our Nation's Highways," American Civil Liberties Union (ACLU) *Special Report*, June 7, 1999.

Hernandez-Murillo, Ruben and Knowles, John (July 2004). "Racial Profiling or Racist Policing? Bounds Tests in Aggregate Data," *International Economic Review*, Volume 45, No. 3, pp. 959–989.

Mauer, Marc, Potler Cathy and Wolf, Richard (1999). "Gender and Justice: Women, Drugs and Sentencing Policy," *The Sentencing Project*, November. (WWW.SentencingProject.org)

Petrocelli, Matthew, Piquero, Alex R. and Smith, Michael R. (2003). "Conflict Theory and Racial Profiling: An Empirical Analysis of Police Traffic Stop Data," *Journal of Criminal Justice*, Volume 31, Issue 1, January–February, pp. 1–11.

Ridgeway, Greg (March 2006). "Assessing the effect of race bias in post-traffic stop outcomes using propensity scores," *Journal of Quantitative Criminology*, Volume 22, Number 1, pp. 1–29.

Rojek, Jeff, Rosenfeld, Richard and Decker, Scott (2004). "The Influence of Driver's Race on Traffic Stops in Missouri," *Police Quarterly*, Vol. 7, No. 1, pp. 126–147.

Weitzer, Ronald and Tuch, Stephen A. (2006). "Perceptions of racial profiling: race, class and personal experience," *Criminology*, Volume 40, Issue 2, March, pp. 435–456.

Weitzer, Ronald and Tuch, Stephen A. (1999). "Race, class, and Perceptions of Discrimination by the Police." *Crime & Delinquency*, Vol. 45, No. 4, pp. 494–507.

Walker, Samuel (2008). "Searching for the Denominator: Problems with Police Traffic Stop Data and an Early Warning System Solution," *Justice Research and Policy*, Vol. 3, No. 1, spring 2001, pp. 63–96.

Williams, Brian N. and Stahl, Michael (2008). "An Analysis of Police Traffic Stops and Searches in Kentucky: A Mixed Method Approach Offering Heuristic and Practical Implications," *Policy Sciences*, Volume 41, No. 3, September, pp. 221–243.

The Police and the Black Male

Elijah Anderson

The police, in the Village-Northton as else-where, represent society's formal, legitimate means of social control.[1] Their role includes protecting law-abiding citizens from those who are not law-abiding, by preventing crime and by apprehending likely criminals. Precisely how the police fulfill the public's expectations is strongly related to how they view the neighborhood and the people who live there. On the streets, color-coding often works to confuse race, age, class, gender, incivility, and criminality, and it expresses itself most concretely in the person of the anonymous black male. In doing their job, the police often become willing parties to this general colorcoding of the public environment, and related distinctions, particularly those of skin color and gender, come to convey definite meanings. Although such coding may make the work of the police more manageable, it may also fit well with their own presuppositions regarding race and class relations, thus shaping officers' perceptions of crime "in the city." Moreover, the anonymous black male is usually an ambiguous figure who arouses the utmost caution and is generally considered dangerous until he proves he is not.

In July 1988, in the area just south of the Village, my own automobile was taken from its parking place on a main thoroughfare. Convinced that a thief had stolen the car, I quickly summoned the police. Within ten minutes of my calling 911 a police car arrived, driven by a middle-aged white officer. He motioned for me to get in. Because the front seat was cluttered with notebooks and papers, I opened the back door and got in on the right-hand side. I introduced myself to Officer John Riley, mentioning that I was a professor, mainly to help establish myself with him. He was courteous, commiserated with me, then asked for the basic information. What time did I park the car? Could a friend or relative have taken it? During our exchanges I said that my family and I were planning a trip to the Midwest the next day to attend a family reunion, and I could feel his empathy. He said he would call in the report right away, and since the case was "hot," meaning the theft had just occurred, there might be a good

1 See Rubinstein (1973); Wilson (1978); Fogelson (1977); Reiss (1971); Bittner (1967); Banton (1964).

chance of getting the car back soon, if not that very night. He then reported the theft and put out a bulletin. Into his radio he said, "Be on the lookout for a maroon 1982 Oldsmobile four-door sedan, heading northwest on Warrington Avenue." Every police car in the city, particularly those in the same district, was thus given a description of my car and would presumably be on the lookout for it. I was pleased with his attention to my misfortune.

As we sat in the patrol car, the officer interviewed me; and I took the opportunity to interview him as well. We spoke about policing the local area, about car thefts, and about the general crime rate. We discussed the characteristics of car thieves, robbers, muggers, and other antisocial persons in the area. I did not tell him I was a sociologist. I think he thought of himself as simply doing his job, treating me as just another victim of local crime—which I was indeed.

During this conversation the police officer seemed to be feeling me out, attempting to get a fix on me as a person, perhaps wondering where I stood politically. At one point we discussed jobs and crime and their relation to one another. Then the officer mentioned the way "he" had messed up this city and how the "big boys" had already gotten to "him." I took this as implicit criticism of the city's black mayor, so I deferred and listened intently, thinking I could learn something about his attitude concerning local city politics. But I also did not want to alienate this person who was trying to find my car. Hence I played along, pointing out that the mayor's stock had declined in the black community, that even many blacks were not satisfied with his performance.

After this conversational give and take, the officer seemed favorably impressed. He appeared genuinely sympathetic with my fear of missing my family reunion. More than once he suggested that I try to forget the theft for now, rent a Lincoln Town Car like his own, and drive to the reunion. I demurred, insisting that I wanted my own car back as soon as possible.

Through our conversation, he seemed to open up and trust me. Then he offered, "Listen, why don't we drive around and see if we can spot your car. Maybe some kids just took it for a joyride and ditched it." I was appreciative and encouraged him, but I stayed in the backseat, wondering where he would take me to look for my car. We headed north through the Village, across Bellwether, and into Northton. After driving up and down a number of the familiar streets of Northton, we headed for "the projects," about a mile northwest of the Village. When I asked why he had chosen to come here, he replied, "This is where they usually take them [cars]." It seemed he had a definite idea who he was talking about. *They* were the thieves, the robbers, the muggers, and generally the people who cause trouble. And they lived in Northton. As we proceeded, we passed numerous street corner groups of young black men, with some young women among them. Many were simply loitering. He knew some of them and greeted them in a familiar way as we slowly drove past. He would wave and say, "Howy' all doin'" in what sounded like affected Black English. By showing this level of familiarity, he let me know he knew the community: it was to some degree his turf.

As we drove through the projects and the neighborhoods of Northton, ostensibly looking for my car, I felt strange—as though I was somehow identified with "the enemy"—though I was safe in the backseat. Also, when a young black man is sitting in a police car, most people perceive him to be in custody, in some kind of trouble, regardless of the real circumstances. This seems to go with the general definition of affairs in the neighborhood—that to be black and male, particularly when young, is to be suspect; that the young man must prove he is law-abiding. Even though I was sitting in the backseat, so that many onlookers might know the officer considered me "safe" or a victim to be aided, this reality goes strongly against the common sense of the community: a young black male is a suspect until he proves he is not. The burden of proof is not easily lifted.

After riding around Northton for about twenty minutes, we met another police car. The driver, who was white, middle-aged, and alone, had stopped at the corner, preparing to make a right-hand turn. My driver turned left onto the same street, and both stopped with the two cars facing in opposite directions. As they exchanged pleasantries, the second policeman kept looking at me with puzzlement. Black male alone in rear seat. Officer Riley felt the need to explain me and said, "Oh, somebody stole his car, and we're out looking for it. It's a maroon '82 Delta 88. The other policeman nodded. The two continued to make small talk, but the second officer could not keep his eyes off me. I felt that if I made a false move he would come after me. In essence the policeman played his role, and I played mine; notwithstanding that I was a victim of crime, my color and gender seemed to outweigh other claims.

Such roles are expected by the young black men of the neighborhood, who have a clear sense of who they are and what they mean to the police. It is from this knowledge that they infer how to act, and how the police will act, believing both must behave according to an elaborate script of the streets. Much of this may be viewed as symbolic display, but it works to maintain a certain ordering of affairs in the public arena.

In the presence of police officers, who clearly have the upper hand, black youths check themselves. They defer to the police or try to avoid them. And some black men, because of their profound distrust of the criminal justice system, say they would never allow a white policeman to arrest them. A young black male told me, "A white policeman would never go out of his way for a black man."

After about fifteen minutes the policemen finished their talk and said their good-byes. Meanwhile I was simply a nonperson, not their equal, and my time and business were clearly secondary in their minds. As we drove slowly up and down the streets, Officer Riley continued to nod, speak, and wave to people. Finally he gave up, saying he was "sorry, but maybe we'll have some luck tonight or tomorrow. I'll stay on it, and hopefully we'll get your car back." He then offered me a ride home, which I gladly accepted. On the way Officer Riley talked about his own misfortunes with theft, attempting to commiserate with me. I saw one of my white colleagues on a street corner near my house, reading a newspaper while waiting for a bus. As the patrol car pulled up to the light, he casually looked over at me, looked away, then looked again with astonishment. "Eli! Is that you? Are you okay? What's the trouble?" I quickly assured him that everything was all right, that I was with the policeman because my car had been stolen. But my colleague looked unconvinced. The light changed, and Officer Riley drove toward my house. He again expressed his regret for my predicament but said he was hopeful. We parted company, and I never saw him again. But the next morning at 9:00 I got a call that my car had been found and I could come and retrieve it.

There are some who charge—and as this account indicates, perhaps with good reason—that the police are primarily agents of the middle class who are working to make the area more hospitable to middle-class people at the expense of the lower classes. It is obvious that the police assume whites in the community are at least middle class and are trustworthy on the streets. Hence the police may be seen primarily as protecting "law-abiding" middle-class whites against anonymous "criminal" black males.

To be white is to be seen by the police—at least superficially—as an ally, eligible for consideration and for much more deferential treatment than that accorded blacks in general. This attitude may be grounded in the backgrounds of the police themselves. Many have grown up in Eastern City's "ethnic" neighborhoods.[2] They may serve what they perceive as their own class and neighborhood interests, which often translates as keeping blacks "in their place"—away from neighborhoods that are socially defined as "white." In trying to do their job, the police appear to engage in an informal policy of monitoring young black men as a means of controlling crime, and often they seem to go beyond the bounds of duty. The following field note shows what pressures and racism young black men in the Village may endure at the hands of the police:

At 8:30 on a Thursday evening in June I saw a police car stopped on a side street near the Village. Beside the car stood a policeman with a young black man. I pulled up behind the police car and waited to see what would happen. When the policeman released the young man, I got out of my car and asked the youth for an interview.

"So what did he say to you when they stopped you? What was the problem?" I asked. "I was just coming around the corner, and he stopped me, asked me what was my name, and all that. And what I had in my bag. And where I was coming from. Where I lived, you know, all the basic stuff, I guess. Then he searched me down and, you know, asked me who were the supposedly tough guys around here? That's

---

2 For an illuminating typology of police work that draws a distinction between "fraternal" and "professional" codes of behavior, see Wilson (1968).

about it. I couldn't tell him who they are. How do I know? Other gang members could, but I'm not from a gang, you know. But he tried to put me in a gang bag, though." "How old are you?" I asked. "I'm seventeen, I'll be eighteen next month." "Did he give any reason for stopping you?" "No, he didn't. He just wanted my address, where I lived, where I was coming from, that kind of thing. I don't have no police record or nothin'. I guess he stopped me on principle, 'cause I'm black." "How does that make you feel?" I asked. "Well, it doesn't bother me too much, you know, as long as I know that I hadn't done nothin', but I guess it just happens around here. They just stop young black guys and ask 'em questions, you know. What can you do?"

On the streets late at night, the average young black man is suspicious of others he encounters, and he is particularly wary of the police. If he is dressed in the uniform of the "gangster," such as a black leather jacket, sneakers, and a "gangster cap," if he is carrying a radio or a suspicious bag (which may be confiscated), or if he is moving too fast or too slow, the police may stop him. As part of the routine, they search him and make him sit in the police car while they run a check to see whether there is a "detainer" on him. If there is nothing, he is allowed to go on his way. After this ordeal the youth is often left afraid, sometimes shaking, and uncertain about the area he had previously taken for granted. He is upset in part because he is painfully aware of how close he has come to being in "big trouble." He knows of other youths who have gotten into a "world of trouble" simply by being on the streets at the wrong time or when the police were pursuing a criminal. In these circumstances, particularly at night, it is relatively easy for one black man to be mistaken for another. Over the years, while walking through the neighborhood I have on occasion been stopped and questioned by police chasing a mugger, but after explaining myself I was released.

Many youths, however, have reason to fear such mistaken identity or harassment, since they might be jailed, if only for a short time, and would have to post bail money and pay legal fees to extricate themselves from the mess (Anderson 1986). When law-abiding blacks are ensnared by the criminal justice system,

the scenario may proceed as follows. A young man is arbitrarily stopped by the police and questioned. If he cannot effectively negotiate with the officer(s), he may be accused of a crime and arrested. To resolve this situation he needs financial resources, which for him are in short supply. If he does not have money for an attorney, which often happens, he is left to a public defender who may be more interested in going along with the court system than in fighting for a poor black person. Without legal support, he may well wind up "doing time" even if he is innocent of the charges brought against him. The next time he is stopped for questioning he will have a record, which will make detention all the more likely.

Because the young black man is aware of many cases when an "innocent" black person was wrongly accused and detained, he develops an "attitude" toward the police. The street word for police is "the man," signifying a certain machismo, power, and authority. He becomes concerned when he notices "the man" in the community or when the police focus on him because he is outside his own neighborhood. The youth knows, or soon finds out, that he exists in a legally precarious state. Hence he is motivated to avoid the police, and his public life becomes severely circumscribed.

To obtain fair treatment when confronted by the police, the young man may wage a campaign for social regard so intense that at times it borders on obsequiousness. As one streetwise black youth said: "If you show a cop that you nice and not a smartass, they be nice to you. They talk to you like the man you are. You gonna get ignorant like a little kid, they gonna get ignorant with you." Young black males often are particularly deferential toward the police even when they are completely within their rights and have done nothing wrong. Most often this is not out of blind acceptance or respect for the "law," but because they know the police can cause them hardship. When confronted or arrested, they adopt a particular style of behavior to get on the policeman's good side. Some simply "go limp" or politely ask, "What seems to be the trouble, officer?" This pose requires a deference that is in sharp contrast with the youths' more usual image, but many seem to take it in stride or not even to realize it. Because they are concerned primarily with staying out of trouble, and because they perceive the police as arbitrary in their use of power, many defer in an equally arbitrary way. Because of these pressures, however, black youths tend to be especially mindful of the police and, when they are around, to watch their own behavior in public. Many have come to expect harassment and are inured to it; they simply tolerate it as part of living in the Village-Northton.

After a certain age, say twenty-three or twenty-four, a black man may no longer be stopped so often, but he continues to be the object of police scrutiny. As one twenty-seven-year-old black college graduate speculated:

> *I think they see me with my little bag with papers in it. They see me with penny loafers on. I have a tie on, some days. They don't stop me so much now. See, it depends on the circumstances. If something goes down, and they hear that the guy had on a big black coat, I may be the one. But when I was younger, they could just stop me, carte blanche, any old time. Name taken, searched, and this went on endlessly. From the time I was about twelve until I was sixteen or seventeen, endlessly, endlessly. And I come from a lower-middle-class black neighborhood, OK, that borders a white neighborhood. One neighborhood is all black, and one is all white. OK, just because we were so close to that neighborhood, we were stopped endlessly. And it happened even more when we went up into a suburban community. When we would ride up and out to the suburbs, we were stopped every time we did it.*
>
> *If it happened today, now that I'm older, I would really be upset. In the old days when I was younger, I didn't know any better. You just expected it, you knew it was gonna happen. Cops would come up, "What you doing, where you coming from?" Say things to you. They might even call you nigger.*

Such scrutiny and harassment by local police makes black youths see them as a problem to get beyond, to deal with, and their attempts affect their overall behavior. To avoid encounters with the man, some streetwise young men camouflage themselves, giving up the urban uniform and emblems that identify them as "legitimate" objects of police attention. They may adopt a more conventional presentation of self, wearing chinos, sweat suits, and generally more conservative dress. Some youths have been known to "ditch" a favorite jacket if they see others wearing one like it, because wearing it increases their chances of being mistaken for someone else who may have committed a crime.

But such strategies do not always work over the long run and must be constantly modified. For instance, because so many young ghetto blacks have begun to wear Fila and Adidas sweat suits as status symbols, such dress has become incorporated into the public image generally associated with young black males. These athletic suits, particularly the more expensive and colorful ones, along with high-priced sneakers, have become the leisure dress of successful drug dealers, and other youths will often mimic their wardrobe to "go for bad" in the quest for local esteem. Hence what was once a "square" mark of distinction approximating the conventions the wider culture has been adopted by a neighborhood group devalued by that same culture. As we saw earlier, the young black male enjoys a certain power over fashion: whatever the collective peer group embraces can become "hip" in a manner the wider society may not desire (see Goffman 1963). These same styles then attract the attention of the agents of social control.

The Identification Card

Law-abiding black people, particularly those of the middle class, set out to approximate middle-class whites in styles of self-presentation in public, including dress and bearing. Such middle class emblems, often viewed as "square," are not usually embraced by young working-class blacks. Instead, their connections with and claims on the institutions of the wider society seem to be symbolized by the identification card. The common identification card associates its holder with a firm, a corporation, a school, a union, or some other institution of substance and influence. Such a card, particularly from a prominent establishment, puts the police and others on notice that the youth is "somebody," thus creating an important distinction between a black man who can claim a connection with the wider society and one who is summarily judged as "deviant." Although blacks who are established in the middle class might take such cards for granted, many lower-class blacks, who continue to find it necessary to campaign for civil rights denied them because of skin color, believe that carrying an identification card brings them better treatment than is meted out to their less fortunate brothers and sisters. For them this link to the wider society, though often tenuous, is psychically and socially important. The young college graduate continues:

> I know [how] I used to feel when I was enrolled in college last year, when I had an ID card. I used to hear stories about the blacks getting stopped over by the dental school, people having trouble sometimes. I would see that all the time. Young black male being stopped by the police. Young black male in handcuffs. But I knew that because I had that ID card I would not be mistaken for just somebody snatching a pocketbook, or just somebody being where maybe I wasn't expected be. See, even though I was intimidated by the campus police—I mean, the first time I walked into the security office to get my ID they

> all gave me the double take to see if I was somebody they were looking for. See, after I got the card, I was like, well, they can think that now, but I have this [ID card]. Like, see, late at night when I be walking around, and the cops be checking me out, giving me the looks, you know. I mean, I know guys, students, who were getting stopped all the time, sometimes by the same officer, even though they had the ID. And even they would say, "Hey, I got the ID, so why was I stopped?"

The cardholder may believe he can no longer be treated summarily by the police, that he is no longer likely to be taken as a "no count," to be prejudicially confused with that class of blacks "who are always causing trouble on the trolley." Furthermore, there is a firm belief that if the police stop a person who has a card, they cannot "do away with him without somebody coming to his defense." This concern should not be underestimated. Young black men trade stories about mistreatment at the hands of the police; a common one involves policemen who transport youths into rival gang territories and release them, telling them to get home the best way they can. From the youth's perspective, the card signifies a certain status in circumstances where little recognition was formerly available.

"Downtown" Police and Local Police

In attempting to manage the police—and by implication to manage themselves—some black youths have developed a working conception of the police in certain public areas of the Village-Northton. Those who spend a good amount of their time on these corners, and thus observing the police, have come to distinguish between the "downtown" police and the "regular" local police.

The local police are the ones who spend time in the area; normally they drive around in patrol cars, often one officer to a car. These officers usually make a kind of working peace with the young men on the streets; for example, they know the names of some of them and may even befriend a young boy. Thus they offer an image of the police department different from that displayed by the "downtown" police.

The downtown police are distant, impersonal, and often actively looking for "trouble." They are known to swoop down arbitrarily on gatherings of black youths standing on a street corner; they might punch them around, call them names, and administer other kinds of abuse, apparently for sport. A young Northton man gave the following narrative about his experiences with the police.

> And I happen to live in a violent part. There's a real difference between the violence level in the Village and the violence level in Northton. In the nighttime it's more dangerous over there.
>
> It's so bad now, they got downtown cops over there now. They doin' a good job bringin' the

highway patrol over there. Regular cops don't like that. You can tell that. They even try to emphasize to us the certain category. Highway patrol come up, he leave, they say somethin' about it. "We can do our job over here." We call [downtown police] Nazis. They about six feet eight, seven feet. We walkin', they jump out. "You run, and we'll blow your nigger brains out."
I hate bein' called a nigger. I want to say somethin' but get myself in trouble.

When a cop do somethin', nothing happen to 'em. They come from downtown. From what I heard some of 'em don't even wear their real badge numbers. So you have to put up with that. Just keep your mouth shut when they stop you, that's all. Forget about questions, get against the wall, just obey 'em. "Put all that out right there"—might get rough with you now. They snatch you by the shirt, throw you against the wall, pat you hard, and grab you by the arms, and say, "Get outta here." They call you nigger this and little black this, and things like that. I take that. Some of the fellas get mad. It's a whole different world.

Yeah, they lookin' for trouble. They gotta look for trouble when you got five, eight police cars together and they laughin' and talkin', start teasin' people. One night we were at a bar, we read in the paper that the downtown cops cornin' to straighten things out. Same night, three police cars, downtown cops with their boots on, they pull the sticks out, heatin' around the corner, chase into bars. My friend Todd, one of 'em grabbed him and knocked the shit out of him. He punched 'im, a little short white guy. They start a riot. Cops started that shit. Everybody start seein' how wrong the cops was—they start throwin' bricks and bottles, cussin' 'em out. They lock my boy up; they had to let him go. He was just standin' on the corner, they snatch him like that.

One time one of 'em took a gun and began hittin' people. My boy had a little hickie from that. He didn't know who the cop was, because there was no such thing as a badge number. They have phony badge numbers. You can tell they're tougher, the way they dress, plus they're bigger. They have boots, trooper pants, blond hair, blue eyes, even black [eyes]. And they seven feet tall, and six foot

six inches and six foot eight inches. Big! They the rough cops. You don't get smart with them or they beat the shit out of you in front of everybody, they don't care.

We call 'em Nazis. Even the blacks among them. They ride along with 'em. They stand there and watch a white cop beat your brains out. What takes me out is the next day you don't see 'em. Never see 'em again, go down there, come back, and they ride right back downtown, come back, do their little dirty work, go back downtown, and put their real badges on. You see 'em with a forty-five or fifty-five number: "Ain't no such number here, I'm sorry, son." Plus, they got unmarked cars. No sense takin' 'em to court. But when that happened at that bar, another black cop from the sixteenth [local] district, ridin' a real car, came back and said, "Why don't y'all go on over to the sixteenth district and file a complaint? Them musclin' cops was wrong. Beatin' people." So about ten people went over there; sixteenth district knew nothin' about it. They come in unmarked cars, they must have been downtown cops. Some of 'em do it. Some of 'em are off duty, on their way home. District commander told us they do that. They have a patrol over there, but them cops from downtown have control of them cops. Have bigger ranks and bigger guns. They carry .357s and regular cops carry little .38s. Downtown cops are all around. They carry magnums.

Two cars the other night. We sittin' on the steps playing cards. Somebody called the cops. We turn around and see four regular police cars and two highway police cars. We drinkin' beer and playin' cards. Police get out and say you're gamblin'. We say we got nothin' but cards here, we got no money. They said all right, got back in their cars, and drove away. Downtown cops dressed up like troopers. That's intimidation. Damn!

You call a cop, they don't come. My boy got shot, we had to take him to the hospital ourselves. A cop said, "You know who did it?" We said no. He said, "Well, I hope he dies if y' all don't say nothin'." What he say that for? My boy said, "I hope your mother die," he told the cop right to his face. And I was grabbin' another cop, and he made a complaint about that. There were a lot of witnesses. Even the nurse behind the counter said the cop had no business saying nothin' like that. He said it loud, "I hope he dies." Nothin' like that should be comin' from a cop.

Such behavior by formal agents of social control may reduce the crime rate, but it raises questions about social justice and civil rights. Many of the old-time liberal white residents of the Village view the police with some ambivalence. They want their streets and homes defended, but many are convinced that the police manhandle "kids" and mete out an arbitrary form of "justice." These feelings make many of them reluctant to call the police when they are needed, and they may even be less than completely cooperative after a crime has been committed. They know that far too often the police simply "go out and pick up some poor black kid." Yet they do cooperate, if ambivalently, with these agents of social control.

In an effort to gain some balance in the emerging picture of the police in the Village-Northton, I interviewed local officers. The following edited conversation with Officer George Dickens (white) helps place in context the fears and concerns of local residents, including black males:

I'm sympathetic with the people who live in this neighborhood [the Village-Northton], who I feel are victims of drugs. There are a tremendous number of decent, hardworking people who are just trying to live their life in peace and quiet, not cause any problems for their neighbors, not cause any problems for themselves. They just go about their own business and don't bother anyone. The drug situation as it exists in Northton today causes them untold problems. And some of the young kids are involved in one way or another with this drug culture. As a result, they're gonna come into conflict even with the police they respect and have some rapport with.

We just went out last week on Thursday and locked up ten young men on Cherry Street, because over a period of about a week, we had undercover police officers making drug buys from those young men. This was very well documented and detailed. They were videotaped selling the drugs. And as a result, right now, if you walk down Cherry Street,

it's pretty much a ghost town; there's nobody out. [Before, Cherry Street was notorious for drug traffic.] Not only were people buying drugs there, but it was a very active street. There's been some shock value as a result of all those arrests at one time.

Now, there's two reactions to that. The [television] reporters went out and interviewed some people who said, "Aw, the police overreacted, they locked up innocent people. It was terrible, it was harassment." One of the neighbors from Cherry Street called me on Thursday, and she was outraged. Because she said, "Officer, it's not fair. We've been working with the district for well over a year trying to solve some of the problems on Cherry Street." But most of the neighbors were thrilled that the police came and locked all those kids up. So you're getting two conflicting reactions here. One from the people that live there that just wanta be left alone, alright? Who are really being harassed by the drug trade and everything that's involved in it. And then you have a reaction from the people that are in one way or another either indirectly connected or directed connected, where they say, "You know, if a young man is selling drugs, to him that's a job." And if he gets arrested, he's out of a job. The family's lost their income. So they're not gonna pretty much want anybody to come in there to make arrests. So you've got contradicting elements of the community there. My philosophy is that we're going to try to make Northton livable. If that means we have to arrest some of the residents of Northton, that's what we have to do.

You talk to Tyrone Pitts, you know the group that they formed was formed because of a reaction to complaints against one of the officers of how the teenagers were being harassed. And it turned out that basically what he [the officer] was doing was harassing drug dealers. When Northton against Drugs actually formed and seemed to jell, they developed a close working relationship with the police here. For that reason, they felt the officer was doing his job.

I've been here eighteen months. I've seen this neighborhood go from ... Let me say, this is the only place I've ever worked where I've seen a rapport between the police department and the general community like the one we have right now. I've never seen it anyplace else before coming here. And I'm not gonna claim credit because this happened while I happened to be here. I think a lot of different factors were involved. I think the community was ready to work with the police because of the terrible situation in reference to crack. My favorite expression when talking about crack is "crack changed everything." Crack changed the rules of how the police and the community have to interact with each other. Crack changed the rules about how the criminal justice system is gonna work, whether it works well or poorly. Crack is causing the prisons to be overcrowded. Crack is gonna cause the people that do drug rehabilitation to be overworked. It's gonna cause a wide variety of things. And I think the reason the rapport between the police and the community in Northton developed at the time it did is very simply that drugs to a certain extent made many areas in this city unlivable.

In effect the officer is saying that the residents, regardless of former attitudes, are now inclined to be more sympathetic with the police and to work with them. And at the same time, the police are more inclined to work with the residents. Thus, not only are the police and the black residents of Northton working together, but different groups in the Village and Northton are working with each other against drugs. In effect, law-abiding citizens are coming together, regardless of race, ethnicity, and class. He continues:

Both of us [police and the community] are willing to say, "Look, let's try to help each other." The nice thing about what was started here is that it's spreading to the rest of the city. If we don't work together, this problem is gonna devour us. It's gonna eat us alive. It's a state of emergency, more or less.

In the past there was significant negative feeling among young black men about the "downtown" cops coming into the community and harassing them. In large part these feelings continue to run strong, though many young men appear to "know the score" and to be resigned to their situation, accommodating and attempting to live with it. But as the general community feels under attack, some residents are willing to forgo certain legal and civil rights and undergo personal inconvenience in hopes of obtaining a sense of law and order. The officer continues:

Today we don't have too many complaints about police harassment in the community. Historically there were these complaints, and in almost any minority neighborhood in Eastern City where I ever worked there was more or less a feeling of that [harassment]. It wasn't just Northton; it was a feeling that the police were the enemy. I can honestly say that for the first time in my career I don't feel that people look at me like I'm the enemy. And it feels nice; it feels real good not to be the enemy, ha-ha. I think we [the police] realize that a lot of the problems here [in the Village-Northton] are related to drugs. I think the neighborhood realizes that too. And it's a matter of "Who are we gonna be angry with? Are we gonna be angry with the police because we feel like they're this army of occupation, or are we gonna argue with these people who are selling drugs to our kids and shooting up our neighborhoods and generally causing havoc in the area? Who deserves the anger more?" And I think, to a large extent, people of the Village-Northton decided it was the drug dealers and not the police.

I would say there are probably isolated incidents where the police would stop a male in an area where there is a lot of drugs, and this guy may be perfectly innocent, not guilty of doing anything at all. And yet he's stopped by the police because he's specifically in that area, on that street corner where we know drugs are going hog wild. So there may be isolated incidents of that. At the same time, I'd say I know for a fact that our complaints against police in this division, the whole division, were down about 45 percent. If there are complaints, if there are instances of abuse by the police, I would expect that our complaints would be going up. But they're not; they're dropping.

Such is the dilemma many Villagers face when they must report a crime or deal in some direct way with the police. Stories about police prejudice against blacks are often traded at Village get-togethers. Cynicism about the effectiveness of the police mixed with community suspicion of their behavior toward blacks keeps middle-class Villagers from embracing the notion that they must rely heavily on the formal means of social control to maintain even the minimum freedom of movement they enjoy on the streets.

Many residents of the Village, especially those who see themselves as the "old guard" or "old-timers," who were around during the good old days when antiwar and antiracist protest was a major concern, sigh and turn their heads when they see the criminal justice system operating in the ways described here. They express hope that "things will work out," that tensions will ease, that crime will decrease and police behavior will improve. Yet as incivility and crime become increasing problems in the neighborhood, whites become less tolerant of anonymous blacks and more inclined to embrace the police as their heroes.

Such criminal and social justice issues, crystallized on the streets, strain relations between the newcomers and many of the old guard, but in the present context of drug-related crime and violence in the Village-Northton, many of the old-timers are adopting a "law and order" approach to crime and public safety, laying blame more directly on those they see as responsible for such crimes, though they retain some ambivalence. Newcomers can share such feelings with an increasing number of old-time "liberal" residents.

As one middle-aged white woman who has lived in the Village for fifteen years said:

> When I call the police, they respond. I've got no complaints. They are fine for me. I know they sometimes mistreat black males. But let's face it, most of the crime is committed by them, and so they can simply tolerate more scrutiny. But that's them.

Gentrifiers and the local old-timers who join them, and some traditional residents continue to fear, care more for their own safety and well-being than for the rights of young blacks accused of wrongdoing. Yet reliance on the police, even by an increasing number of former liberals, may be traced to a general feeling of oppression at the hands of street criminals, whom many believe are most often black. As these feelings intensify and as more yuppies and students inhabit the area and press the local government for services, especially police protection, the police may be required to "ride herd" more stringently on the youthful black population. Thus young black males are often singled out as the "bad" element in an otherwise healthy diversity, and the tensions between the lower-class black ghetto and the middle and upper-class white community increase rather than diminish.

REFERENCES

Anderson, Elijah. 1986. Of old heads and young boys: Notes on the urban black experience. Unpublished paper commissioned by the National Research Council, Committee on the Status of Black Americans.

Banton, Michael. 1964. *The policeman and the community.* New York: Basic Books.

Bittner, Egon. 1967. The police on Skid Row. *American Sociological Review* 32(October): 699–715.

Fogelson, Robert. 1977. *Big city police.* Cambridge: Harvard University Press.

Goffman, Erving. 1963. *Behavior in public places.* New York: Free Press.

Reiss, Albert J. 1971. *The police and the public.* New Haven: Yale University Press.

Rubinstein, Jonathan. 1973. *City police.* New York: Farrar, Straus and Giroux.

Wilson, James Q. 1968. The police and the delinquent in two cities. In *Controlling delinquents,* ed. Stanton Wheeler. New York: John Wiley.

The Influence of Race/ Ethnicity

on the Perceived Prevalence and Support for Racial Profiling at Airports

Shaun L. Gabbidon, Everette B. Penn, Kareem L. Jordan, and George E. Higgins

Racial profiling is defined as the targeting of citizens, based on their race or ethnicity, for additional scrutiny by criminal justice officials. In his recent book on the topic, Alex del Carmen (2008), after reviewing American history, has noted that such practices are not new; today, such practices are simply done in a different way under different circumstances. Notably, in the past two decades, the most recent form of racial profiling has been discovered by social scientists. Because of both the outrage over profiling practices during traffic stops and the resulting litigation targeted at offending law enforcement agencies, state and local governments started requiring officers to track their traffic stops. Consequently, local, state, and federal agencies started to fund studies focused on collecting and analyzing such data. Moreover, the Bureau of Justice Statistics now periodically releases reports highlighting traffic stop data (Smith & Durose, 2006). The tragic events of September 11, 2001, spurred the more recent furor over the racial profiling of Arab Americans, people of Middle Eastern descent, and Muslims (Onwudiwe, 2005). Nonetheless, the bulk of the scholarly literature on racial profiling is devoted to research that focuses on either actual traffic stops or public opinion on this form of racial profiling (Holbert & Rose, 2004; Milovanovic & Russell-Brown, 2001; Withrow, 2006). This article diverges from this trend and centers on public opinion related to profiling at airports.

Authors' Note: The authors thank Dr. Mukund Kulkarni at Penn State Harrisburg for research support that was instrumental in securing the data used in this article.

Historical Background on Airport/Airline Security

Just as racial profiling is not a new practice, concerns about airport and airline security are also not new. In fact, nearly 80 years ago, in 1930, the first recorded airplane hijacking occurred when "Peruvian revolutionaries seized a Pan American mail plane and used it to drop propaganda leaflets over Lima" (Trento & Trento, 2006, p. 56). The 1940s also saw cold war hijackings by those trying to escape the iron curtain. The 1950s saw other types of attacks on airlines, with the case of Jack Graham being most notable. In hopes of collecting money on an insurance policy, the FBI learned that Graham had placed a bomb in his mother's suitcase. When the bomb detonated, his mother and the other 43 passengers on the plane were killed (Trento & Trento, 2006).

Following these early incidents, the 1960s and 1970s represented the period when some of the earliest concerns about airline security were expressed. During this period, hijackings were often tied to terrorist activities and political upheavals across the globe. In fact, in 1969, because of these concerns Congress directed the Federal Aviation Administration to study airline hijacking and devise ways to prevent them (Fenello, 1971). This direct action was more than justified considering that between 1968 and 1972 there were 364 hijackings (Trento & Trento, 2006). Through the institution of a variety of measures, including the hiring of the first federal air marshals, the inspection of carry-on baggage, the mandatory screening of all passengers, and the use of X-ray devices, the industry was able to turn hijackings into relatively infrequent events (Conarroe, 1974) as there were only four of them in 1976 (Harris, 2002).

One additional tactic used in the 1970s to tackle airline hijackings was the creation of the hijacker profile. This profile was based on the characteristics of all known hijackers (Harris, 2002). The profile was behavioral in nature and did not include racial or ethnic traits.

Once someone fit the characteristics of the profile, their boarding pass was marked, and "in the boarding area, officials screened all passengers with magnetometers … only those who both set off the detector and had a marked boarding pass were singled out for further inquiry" (Harris, 2002, pp. 17–18). Although the profile did minimally reduce the number of hijackings, it was the move to mandatory screening of all passengers and the use of X-ray machines that some believe made the biggest difference (Harris, 2002).

Since September 11, 2001, the allegations regarding racial profiling on the highways has been extended to airports. Arab Americans, people of Middle Eastern descent, and Muslims have expressed the belief that they are being targeted for additional scrutiny at airports (Elliot, 2006; Halter, 2002) and elsewhere (Kazemi, del Carmen, Dobbs, & Whitehead, 2008). Whether this was true has been subject to debate, but things have changed a bit as the airline security concerns of the 1960s and 1970s subsided (Persico & Todd, 2005). Today, for example, there are 97 United States airline carriers that transport more than 650 million passengers each year, and because of security concerns, there are more than 1,000 screening points that handle in excess of 2.5 billion pieces of luggage (Szyliowicz, 2004). Taking into consideration that so many people and pieces of luggage pass through airports everyday, it could be that security personnel use profiles to direct their efforts. Again, to the authors' knowledge, there has not been any evidence to support this supposition, but one wonders whether citizens believe such practices exist and how widespread they might be. In addition, given the monumental task of providing security to millions of passengers each year, one also wonders whether citizens will view racial profiling at airports as being justified. To answer these important questions, this research analyzed data from a recent national Gallup poll. In the following section, public opinion on race and policing and racial profiling are reviewed.

Literature Review

Public opinion research related to criminal justice has a long history (Flanagan & Longmire, 1996). Some of the earliest race-related public opinion research examined the general fairness by which justice was distributed as well as public perception as to whether crime was increasing or decreasing in the Black community (see

Du Bois, 1904; Gabbidon, 2000). Following early public opinion research on this topic, scholars have continued to explore whether racial and ethnic minorities believe they get a fair shake in the criminal justice system. More often then not, Blacks have expressed the belief that they are unfairly treated by criminal justice officials (see Brunson, 2007; Jones-Brown, 2007; Stewart, 2007), whereas, on the other hand, Whites are less likely to have such views (Flanagan & Longmire, 1996; Hagan & Albonetti, 1982). Furthermore, research on Hispanics from more than two decades ago found that the police were perceived to have a bad attitude and discriminated against Hispanics (Carter, 1985). Martinez (2007) has recently called for additional research on Latinos (and immigrants) and the police. We review public opinion research on race and the police below.

PUBLIC OPINION RESEARCH ON RACE AND THE POLICE

In 1967, the president's Commission on Law Enforcement and the Administration of Justice commissioned the National Opinion Research Center to conduct a survey on the public's views toward the police. The results of the survey noted that most of the public felt the police did a very good or excellent job of protecting people. Blacks, however, were less likely to give the police such high marks, and they were also more likely than Whites to feel that the police did not treat them with respect (Gabbidon & Greene, 2009). Since this landmark study, researchers have continued to gauge citizen satisfaction and confidence with the police. In so doing, they have noted differences in perceptions based on race and ethnicity.

In recent years, scholars have not only looked at general public opinion on the police but they have also examined a variety of other aspects of the relationship. Tuch and Weitzer (1997), for example, have noted that, following high-profile police brutality incidents (e.g., Rodney King, O. J. Simpson trial), the support for the police does diminish. In a study of Cincinnati residents, Henderson, Cullen, Cao, Browning, and Kopache (1997) found that race matters in how Blacks and Whites view the criminal justice system. Blacks had a clear sense that the criminal justice system was unfair. Weitzer and Tuch (1999) examined the role of race and class on the perceptions of discrimination by the police. In every area, Blacks saw the performance of the police in a more negative light than Whites (see also Weitzer, 2000).

Expanding the nature of attitudinal studies regarding attitudes toward the police, Escholtz, Sims Blackwell, Gertz, and Chircos (2002) conducted research that explored the possible influence that watching television news and reality crime programs (e.g., Cops) might have on racial attitudes toward the police. Their research found that watching such shows did impact on the views of Whites and Blacks. Weitzer and Tuch (2004a) also examined the role of race, mass media, and neighborhood conditions on the perceptions of the prevalence of police misconduct. Results from their national study found that race was a strong predictor of views toward police misconduct. Their research suggested that the views of Blacks and Hispanics were colored by their "personal and vicarious experience with police misconduct, and to report that they have been the recipients of frequent abuse" (Weitzer & Tuch, 2004a, p. 320). In general, Hispanics' views tended to be situated between those of Blacks and Whites. Neighborhood conditions were also a significant predictor as to whether respondents felt that police misconduct was prevalent in their community (Weitzer & Tuch, 2004a). In another paper, Weitzer and Tuch (2004b) sought to determine if there were racial differences in public support for policy changes related to police practices. Here again, there were differences by race, with Whites being less likely than Blacks and Hispanics to support preferences in hiring to diversify police forces; Blacks and Hispanics are more likely than Whites to believe that hiring more minorities and placing them in minority communities would improve policing where they reside. Also, negative experiences with the police did not affect whether respondents supported police reforms.

It is notable that public opinion research conducted in the mid-1990s in heavily populated inner cities with Black leadership in government and policing revealed that, in contrast to national poll data, Whites had less favorable views of the police than Blacks (Frank, Brandl, Cullen, & Stichman, 1996). To contextualize their findings, the authors noted that, in such cities, as Whites were now the minority group, "they hold attitudes previously reserved for 'minority'-group members" (Frank et al., 1996, p. 332). Furthermore, it was felt that White residents were likely resistant to this new Black power and, as a result, they show their resentment by expressing negative sentiments toward the police.

Although this literature sheds some light on the schism between the views of racial and ethnic minorities and Whites on the nature and level of discriminatory treatment in the criminal justice system, only within the past decade have polls directly asked citizens about their attitudes and experiences concerning racial profiling. This limited literature is reviewed next.

PUBLIC OPINION ON RACIAL PROFILING

One of the earliest papers that analyzed poll data specifically on racial profiling was conducted by Weitzer and Tuch (2002), who made use of a 1999 Gallup poll that queried respondents on three critical areas related to racial profiling. First, the poll sought to determine how frequently the respondents felt the practice occurred (e.g., widespread or not). Second, the poll investigated whether the respondents approved of racial profiling. Lastly, the poll asked about the respondents' personal experiences as to whether they believed they had been previously racially profiled. As one might expect, Blacks (81.6%) were more likely than Whites (60.2%) to believe the practice was widespread (Weitzer & Tuch, 2002). On the second question, very few Blacks (5.7%) or Whites (15.6%) felt the use of racial profiling was appropriate. The final question also produced some interesting findings. Here, Blacks (40%) reported that they had personally experienced racial profiling more than Whites (5%). The other interesting finding here was that when Weitzer and Tuch examined the responses by age, 72.7% of the young Black males (ages 18-34) expressed the feeling that they had been profiled in the past (Weitzer & Tuch, 2002).

Moving beyond the views of Blacks and Whites, the 2001 *New York Times* New York Police Department poll also captured the views of Hispanics on racial profiling. Reitzel, Rice, and Piquero (2004) analyzed data from the poll and noted that Blacks were more likely than other groups to believe that racial profiling was widespread. As with Weitzer and Tuch's findings, Blacks were also more likely than other groups to believe that racial profiling was not justified and, more so than other groups, to feel that they had been the targets of racial profiling (Reitzel et al., 2004; Rice & Piquero, 2005; Rice, Reitzel, & Piquero, 2005). In terms of Hispanics, the authors found that "Hispanic respondents were more likely than non-Hispanics to believe that profiling was widespread and that they had been profiled" (p. 614). Further analysis of the poll also found that the respondents' views of the New York City Police Department (NYPD) were influenced by how they felt about the prevalence and justification of racial profiling (Reitzel & Piquero, 2006).

To further investigate public views on racial profiling, Weitzer and Tuch (2005) conducted a national poll of nearly 1,800 people. Covering some familiar ground, the authors found that Blacks (90%) were more likely than Hispanics (83%) and Whites (70%) to believe that racial profiling was widespread. The authors again also found little support for the belief that racial profiling by the police was justified. Lastly, in concert with their previous findings, Blacks (37%), more so than Hispanics (23%) and Whites (1%), felt they had been stopped by the police solely based of their race (Weitzer & Tuch, 2005).

Current Study

Building on past public opinion research on racial and ethnic profiling, this research examined public opinion on citizens' views concerning airport racial profiling (ARP). In more recent times, as noted previously, the events of September 11, 2001, have renewed concerns regarding security at airports. As such, this research sought to investigate three key questions. First, whether the public perceives that ARP is a significant problem. Second, whether citizens felt the practice of ARP is justified. Finally, does one's race or ethnicity influence public opinion on ARP? These questions are critical because they will help determine whether the public's views concerning racial profiling during traffic stops aligns with their views concerning the practice at airports. In short, does the public believe that, because of the high stakes involved in terrorist attacks on airplanes, the practice is widespread and justified? Moreover, as with public opinion related to racial profiling during traffic stops, do the views of racial and ethnic minorities diverge from those of Whites? Given the heavy emphasis on airport security by the Transportation Security Administration (TSA), answering these questions will help determine whether there is a sense of unfairness regarding the procedures being used to prevent terrorism. Such a finding has the potential to undermine the perceived legitimacy of those carrying out the important function of airport security.

To investigate public opinion on ARP, two hypotheses were formulated. It was hypothesized that racial and ethnic minorities would be more likely than Whites to view ARP as being widespread. This supposition was formulated based on the results from previous public opinion polls in which it was apparent that racial and ethnic minorities had different views than Whites on criminal justice practices. The previously reviewed research showed that Blacks and Hispanics were more likely than Whites to see profiling as being widespread. It is anticipated that this sentiment will hold true for airports despite the fact that, in post September 11, 2001, most of the complaints regarding ARP have come from Arab Americans, persons of Middle Eastern descent, and Muslims.

Second, it was hypothesized that racial and ethnic minorities would be less likely than Whites to view ARP as being justified. Because Whites are less likely to be the targets of racial profiling (Gabbidon & Greene, 2009; Gabbidon & Higgins, 2008; Walker, Spohn, & De Lone, 2007), it stands to reason that they will be more likely than racial or ethnic minorities, who are typically the targets of such practices (Harris, 2002), to believe it is justified. In some ways, this is likely tied to either one's own personal experience encountering racial profiling or having heard that a friend or relative also had such an encounter. Notably, past polls have found a discrepancy between Blacks and Whites when it comes to knowing someone who has been physically mistreated by the police. A 1991 Gallup poll found that 40% of Blacks in comparison to 17% of Whites knew someone who had encountered such treatment (Gallup, 1991). In addition, as noted in the previously reviewed public opinion research, racial and ethnic minorities apparently feel, more so than Whites, that they have been the target of racial profiling. Consequently, they will be less likely to believe it is justified.

Method

The data for this research are taken from the 2004 Minority Rights and Relations/Black-White Social Audit poll conducted from June 9–29, 2004, by the Gallup Organization.[1] Every few years the Gallup organization examines the perceptions of Whites and racial and ethnic minorities concerning a host of social issues. The 2004 poll included more than 2,000 randomly selected Americans, which includes an oversample of Hispanics ($n = 500$) and Blacks ($n = 800$). However, due to extremely small numbers for the Other race category, we included only Blacks, Hispanics, and Whites for this study, resulting in a final sample size of 1,825 respondents. It is noted here that the use of the oversampling required the use of sampling weights so as to not distort the representation and allow for generalizable results. That is, it can be said with 95% confidence that the maximum margin of error is 5%. Therefore, the sample is representative of the United States.

DEPENDENT VARIABLES

There were two dependent variables utilized in this research. First, respondents were asked whether they believed ARP was widespread when stopping passengers at airport security checkpoints (*widespread* = 1; *not widespread* = 0). The second dependent variable examined whether respondents believed ARP was justified when stopping passengers at airport security checkpoints (*yes* = 1; *no* = 0).

INDEPENDENT/CONTROL VARIABLES

There were three race/ethnicity variables: Black, White, and Hispanic. Following past public opinion research on racial profiling, the authors included the following control variables: age (was measured continuously), gender (*male* = 1), income (measured in five ordinal categories), employment status (*employed* = 1), education (measured in four ordinal categories ranging from less than high school to postgraduate), marital status (*married* = 1), type of area respondents lived (urban, rural, or suburban), political ideology (measured in five ordinal categories ranging from very conservative to very liberal), and region of the country based on United States census classifications (i.e., South, East, Midwest, or West). To expand on the previous literature, the authors sought to determine whether having children enrolled in school (*yes* = 1) or being religious (captured through an item which asked how often they attended church; measured in five ordinal categories, ranging from never to once a week) influenced one's views on the topic.

Results

Table 1.3.1 presents descriptive statistics of all the variables employed in the current study.[2] Due to each dependent variable being measured as a dichotomy, logistic regression was chosen as the appropriate method of estimation for multivariate analyses (Menard, 2002).

As can be seen in Table 1.3.2, the first hypothesis was partially supported. Blacks were significantly more likely than Whites to believe that ARP is widespread ($b = .34$; $p < .01$). There was no significant difference, however, between Hispanics and Whites ($b = .29$; $p = .09$), although the coefficient was close to reaching statistical significance.

Two other factors also reached statistical significance in the model. Age had a significant and negative impact: As respondents' age increased, beliefs in ARP being widespread decreased. In addition, political ideology was significant. The more liberal the respondents, the more likely they are to believe that ARP is widespread. The pseudo r-squares indicate that the model explains between 4% and 6% of the variance in the dependent variable. Table 1.3.3 examines Hypothesis 2, which was supported. Both Blacks ($b = -.78$; $p < .01$) and Hispanics ($b = -.41$; $p < .05$) were significantly less likely than Whites to believe that ARP is justified.

There were several other significant factors in the model. Males were more likely than females to believe ARP is justified. Those who have children in school were more likely to believe that ARP is justified as compared to those who do not have children in school. In addition, the more liberal the respondents' ideology, the less likely they were to believe that ARP is justified. Finally, those who live in the suburbs were less likely to believe that ARP is justified, as compared to those who live in urban areas. The pseudo r-squares indicate that the model explains between 5% and 7% of the variance in the dependent variable.

Discussion

This article set out to examine a new area of public opinion research focused on racial profiling at airports. More specifically, two hypotheses guided the investigation into the nuances of citizens' views on ARP. First, it was hypothesized that racial and ethnic minorities would be more likely than Whites to view ARP as being widespread. This hypothesis was only partially supported. Blacks did have different views than Whites. However, the views of Hispanics aligned more with those of Whites than Blacks. It could be that, in contrast to the stated supposition, because Blacks have been the central targets of profiling that occurs on the highways and in retail settings, they are more likely to view ARP as being widespread (see Gabbidon & Higgins, 2008). On the other hand, as Hispanics, and to an even lesser extent Whites, tend not to be targeted for profiling, they are less likely to be the targets of such practices. Consequently, they do not see it as

TABLE 1.3.1 **Descriptive Statistics for All Variables**

Variable	M	SD	Min.	Max.
Age	45.82	16.51	18.00	99.00
Gender (*Male* = 1)	0.42	0.49	0.00	1.00
Black	0.41	0.49	0.00	1.00
White	0.47	0.50	0.00	1.00
Hispanic	0.12	0.32	0.00	1.00
Married	0.47	0.50	0.00	1.00
Employed	0.60	0.49	0.00	1.00
Children in school	0.34	0.47	0.00	1.00
Urban	0.47	0.50	0.00	1.00
Rural	0.14	0.35	0.00	1.00
Suburban	0.39	0.49	0.00	1.00
South	0.44	0.50	0.00	1.00
East	0.17	0.38	0.00	1.00
Midwest	0.15	0.35	0.00	1.00
West	0.25	0.43	0.00	1.00
ARP widespread	0.60	0.49	0.00	1.00
ARP justified	0.25	0.43	0.00	1.00

	n	%
Income categories		
Less than US$20,000	354	18.6
US$20,001–US$30,000	336	17.6
US$30,001–US$50,000	504	26.4
US$50,001–US$75,000	320	16.8
US$75,001+	392	20.6
Education categories		
High school or less	809	39.9
Some college	546	26.9
College graduate	335	16.5
Postgraduate	337	16.6
Church attendance categories		
Never	251	12.5
Seldom	443	22.1
Once a month	313	15.6
Almost every week	277	13.8
Once a week	720	35.9
Political ideology categories		
Very conservative	175	8.7
Conservative	551	27.4
Moderate	797	39.7
Liberal	334	16.6
Very liberal	153	7.6

Note: Min. = Minimum; max. = maximum; ARP = airport racial profiling.

TABLE 1.3.2 **Logistic Regression Estimates of ARP Being Widespread (*n* = 1,731)**

Variable	*B*	SE	Wald	Exp(*B*)
Age	−.01**	.00	15.03	0.99
Gender (*Male* = 1)	−.06	.10	0.39	0.94
Black	.34**	.12	8.40	1.40
Hispanic	.29	.17	2.87	1.33
Married	−.14	.11	1.37	0.88
Employed	.00	.11	0.00	1.00
Education	.04	.05	0.58	1.04
Income	−.02	.05	0.13	0.98
Children in school	.10	.11	0.79	1.10
Political ideology	.21**	.05	17.96	1.24
Church attendance	.03	.04	0.74	1.03
Suburban	−.18	.11	2.61	0.84
Rural	−.23	.16	2.10	0.80
East	.03	.15	0.05	1.04
Midwest	−.15	.15	0.96	0.86
West	.19	.13	2.02	1.21
Constant	−.22	.31	0.50	0.80
−2 Log likelihood	2,326.21			
Model chi-square	72.98**			
Cox and Snell R^2	.04			
Nagelkerke R^2	.06			

Note: ARP = Airport racial profiling.

being a widespread problem. One additional note here relates to the finding that as age increased the belief that ARP was widespread decreased. As noted in the literature review, age has mattered in terms of public opinion on racial profiling (Weitzer & Tuch, 2002). As young people tend to believe they are the targets of racial profiling, they are also more likely to express the view that profiling—in any context—is widespread.

The finding that Blacks and Hispanics were less likely than Whites to believe the practice of racial profiling at airports was justified supported the second hypothesis. Here again, experience might matter. Past public opinion research on racial profiling occurring during traffic stops has suggested that, given the fact that racial and ethnic minorities tend to believe they have experienced such profiling (Reitzel, Rice, & Piquero, 2004) more than Whites, they are less likely

to the view the practice as being justified—irrespective of the setting.

As for the results from the control variables in the model, it was a bit surprising that the more religious one was, the more likely they felt profiling was justified. One would think that those who attend church most frequently would have an ideal view of the world in which practices such as racial profiling—in which race is used to single out persons for additional scrutiny—would go against religious teachings. However, as has been witnessed in the United States and across the globe, religion is not always associated with peace and nonviolence. The finding that those persons with children were more likely to believe ARP was justified suggests that they might be fearful for the safety of their children and therefore approve of the practice. This finding is consistent with earlier research that

TABLE 1.3.3 **Logistic Regression Estimates of ARP Justification (n = 1,825)**

Variable	B	SE	Wald	Exp(B)
Age	.00	.00	0.00	1.00
Gender (*Male* = 1)	.36**	.10	12.40	1.43
Black	−.78**	.12	44.95	0.46
Hispanic	−.41*	.17	6.04	0.66
Married	.08	.11	0.51	1.08
Employed	−.04	.11	0.13	0.96
Education	.03	.05	0.24	1.03
Income	.02	.05	0.14	1.02
Children in school	.32**	.11	8.63	1.38
Political ideology	−.15**	.05	9.22	0.86
Church attendance	.00	.04	0.01	1.00
Suburban	−.22*	.11	4.09	0.80
Rural	−.11	.16	0.49	0.90
East	.07	.15	0.20	1.07
Midwest	.13	.15	0.79	1.14
West	.06	.13	0.21	1.06
Constant	.12	.31	0.15	1.13
−2 Log likelihood	2,376.73			
Model chi-square	100.68**			
Cox and Snell R^2	.05			
Nagelkerke R^2	.07			

Note: ARP = Airport racial profiling.

*p < .05. **p < .01.

found large numbers of young minorities who felt they had been targeted for racial profiling (Weitzer & Tuch, 2002). The significant finding regarding suburban respondents might be a function of the fact that suburbanites are more likely to travel and are less likely to be minorities, who tend to be the targets of profiling in general; therefore, they are more likely than urban or rural residents to believe that ARP is justified. Each of these variables has received minimal attention in previous public opinion research on racial profiling. Given these findings, it is apparent that researchers need to attempt to better understand their meaning.

In sum, the emphasis on airport security clearly took on additional significance after September 11, 2001. However, as noted earlier, the concern regarding airport and airline security is longstanding. The difficulty today, however, is balancing the safety and security of the American public while maintaining civil liberties.

Study Limitations

Though this research provided some interesting insights into the public's views on a newer aspect of the racial profiling dialogue, it was not without limitation. First, the data were cross-sectional, which does not allow for the researcher to track the respondents' views over time. It might be that respondents' views will change after either experiencing ARP or witnessing someone else fall victim to the practice. Thus, to capture such changes, a longitudinal design would be required. Second, the data set oversampled Blacks and Hispanics but did not have any substantial number of Asian Americans or Native Americans. One wonders whether their views would align with those of other racial ethnic minorities or of Whites. Finally, there were very few Arab Americans, people of Middle Eastern descent, or Muslims in the Gallup data set. Capturing the views of these people would have been useful for gauging the perceived nature of the problem through the eyes of those groups that have been the alleged targets of ARP.

Conclusion

This research set out to explore public opinion on racial profiling at airports. The research showed support for two hypotheses related to whether citizens view such profiling as being widespread and or justified. Considering that 60% of the respondents felt that ARP was widespread, this research should be of concern to policy makers. Although there is no evidence to support these perceptions, the fact that the public feels this way suggests that the TSA should examine its practices to ensure that this perception is not a reality. As for the finding regarding ARP being justified, nearly a quarter of the respondents supported the practice. Another major terrorist attack spearheaded by foreign terrorists on American soil could produce a compelling argument by some to use race/ethnicity as one of the critical factors in identifying terrorists. This would be a break from the successful practices of the 1970s that excluded race/ethnicity from their efforts to minimize hijackings. Finally, based on the results herein, racial and ethnic minorities are clearly less likely to support such a change in policy. To do so, from their perspective, might produce an open season on them being the targets of profiling.

This research provides a launching point for additional research to better understand public opinion on security measures being taken to prevent terrorism. Moreover, given the widespread concerns surrounding security at airports, researchers need to investigate not only the views concerning racial profiling at airports but also find ways to study the actual prevalence of such profiling. In short, just as researchers have investigated nearly every aspect of racial profiling in automobiles, they need to also devote scholarly attention to profiling at airports, as it pertains to preventing terrorism and protecting the homeland.

NOTES

1. The data were obtained directly from the Gallup Organization.
2. We also checked for collinearity between the independent variables. The tolerance and variance inflation factor values indicated the collinearity was not a salient concern, as all of the tolerance scores were greater than 4 and none of the variance inflation factor (VIF) values exceeded 2.5 (see Kutner, Nachtsheim, Neter, & Li, 2005; Mernard, 2002).

REFERENCES

Brunson, R. K. (2007). "Police don't like Black people": African-American young men's accumulated police experiences. *Criminology & Public Policy, 6*, 71–102.

Carter, D. (1985). Hispanic perceptions of police performance. *Journal of Criminal Justice, 13*, 487–500.

Conarroe, M. T. (1974). Law enforcement essential to air safety. *Police Chief, 41*(2), 22–24.

Del Carmen, A. (2008). *Racial profiling in America.* Upper Saddle River, NJ: Pearson/Prentice Hall.

Du Bois, W. E. B. (1904). (Ed.). *Some notes on Negro crime, particularly in Georgia.* Atlanta, GA: Atlanta University Press.

Elliot, A. (2006). After 9/11 Arab-Americans fear police acts, study finds. *New York Times.* Retrieved on April 12, 2008, from http://www.nytimes.com/2006/06/12/us/12arabs.html?_r=1&oref=slogin

Eschholz, S., Sims Blackwell, B., Gertz, M., & Chiricos, T. (2002). Race and attitudes towards the police: Assessing the effects of watching "reality" police programs. *Journal of Criminal Justice, 30,* 327-341.

Fenello, M. J. (1971). *Technical Prevention of Air Piracy.* New York: Carnegie Endowment for International Peace.

Flanagan, T. J., & Longmire, D. R. (Eds.). (1996). *Americans view crime and justice: A national public opinion survey.* Thousand Oaks, CA: Sage.

Frank, J., Brandl, S. G., Cullen, F. T., & Stichman, A. (1996). Reassessing the impact of race of citizens' attitudes toward the police: A research note. *Justice Quarterly, 2,* 321-334.

Gabbidon, S. L. (2000). An early American crime poll by W. E. B. Du Bois. *Western Journal of Black Studies, 24,* 167-174.

Gabbidon, S. L., & Greene, H. T. (2009). *Race and Crime* (2nd ed.). Thousand Oaks, CA: Sage.

Gabbidon, S. L., & Higgins, G. E. (2007). Consumer racial profiling and perceived victimization: A phone survey of Philadelphia area residents. *American Journal of Criminal Justice, 32,* 1-11.

Gabbidon, S. L., & Higgins, G. E. (2008). Profiling White Americans: A research note on "shopping while *White.*" In Michael J. Lynch, E. Britt Patterson, & Kristina Childs (Eds.), *Racial divide: Race, ethnicity and criminal justice.* Monsey, NY: Criminal Justice Press.

Gallup. (1991). *The Gallup poll: Public opinion 1991.* Wilmington, DE: Gallup Organization.

Hagan, J., & Albonetti, C. (1982). Race, class, and the perception of criminal injustice in America. *American Journal of Sociology, 88,* 329-355.

Halter, K. (2002). Flying while brown. *Washington Report on Middle East Affairs, 21,* 85-86.

Harris, D. A. (2002). *Profiles in injustice: Why racial profiling cannot work.* New York: The New Press.

Henderson, M. L., Cullen, F. T., Cao, L., Browning, S. L., & Kopache, R. (1997). The impact of race on perceptions of criminal injustice. *Journal of Criminal Justice, 25,* 447-462.

Holbert, S., & Rose, L. (2004). *The color of guilt & innocence: Racial profiling and police practices in America.* San Ramon, CA: Page Marque Press.

Jones-Brown, D. (2007). Forever the symbolic assailant: The more things change, the more they stay the same. *Criminology & Public Policy, 6,* 103-122.

Kazemi, M. F., del Carmen, A., Dobbs, R. R., & Whitehead, M. (2008). Muslim American perspectives of the global war on terror: An exploratory analysis. *Criminal Justice Studies, 21,* 95-108.

Kutner, M. H., Nachtsheim, C. J., Neter, J., & Li, W. (2005). *Applied linear statistical models* (5th ed.). New York: McGraw-Hill/Irwin.

Martinez, R. (2007). Incorporating Latinos and immigrants into policing research. *Criminology & Public Policy, 6,* 57-64.

Menard, S. (2002). *Applied logistic regression analysis* (2nd ed.). Thousand Oaks, CA: Sage.

Milovanovic, D., & Russell-Brown, K. (Eds.). (2001). *Petit apartheid in the U.S. criminal justice system.* Durham, NC: Carolina Academic Press.

Onwudiwe, I. D. (2005). Defining terrorism, racial profiling and the demonisation of Arabs and Muslims in the USA. *Community Safety Journal, 4,* 4-11.

Persico, N., & Todd, P. E. (2005). Passenger profiling, imperfect screening, and airport security. *American Economic Review, 95,* 127-131.

Rice, S., & Piquero, A. R. (2005). Perceptions of racial profiling and justice: Does race matter. *Policing, 28,* 98-117.

Reitzel, J., & Piquero, A. R. (2006). Does it exist? Studying citizens' attitudes of racial profiling. *Police Quarterly, 9,* 161-183.

Reitzel, J., Rice, S. K., & Piquero, A. R. (2004). Lines and shadows: Perceptions of racial profiling and the Hispanic experience. *Journal of Criminal Justice, 32,* 607-616.

Rice, S. K., Reitzel, J. D., & Piquero, A. R. (2005). Shades of brown: Perception of racial profiling and the intra-ethnic differential. *Journal of Ethnicity in Criminal Justice, 3,* 47-70.

Smith, E. L., & Durose, M. R. (2006). *Characteristics of drivers stopped by the police, 2002.* Washington, DC: Bureau of Justice Statistics.

Stewart, E. A. (2007). Either they don't know or they don't care: Black males and negative police experiences. *Criminology & Public Policy, 6,* 123-130.

Szyliowicz, J. S. (2004). Aviation security: Promise or reality? *Studies in Conflict and Terrorism, 27,* 47-63.

Trento, S. B., & Trento, J. J. (2006). *Unsafe at any altitude: Failed terrorism investigations, scapegoating 9/11, and the shocking truth about aviation security today.* Hanover, NH: Steerforth Press.

Tuch, S. A., & Weitzer, R. (1997). The polls—trends: Racial differences in attitudes toward the police. *Public Opinion Quarterly, 61,* 642-663.

Walker, S., Spohn, C., & DeLone, M. (2007). *The color of justice: Race, ethnicity, and crime in America.* Belmont, CA: Thomson/Wadsworth.

Weitzer, R. (2000). Racialized policing: Residents' perceptions in three neighborhoods. *Law & Society Review, 34,* 129-155.

Weitzer, R., & Tuch, S. A. (1999). Race, class, and perceptions of discrimination by the police. *Crime & Delinquency, 45,* 435-456.

Weitzer, R., & Tuch, S. A. (2002). Perceptions of racial profiling: Race, class, and personal experience. *Criminology, 40,* 435-456.

Weitzer, R., & Tuch, S. A. (2004a). Race and perceptions of misconduct. *Social Problems, 51,* 305-325.

Weitzer, R., & Tuch, S. A. (2004b). Reforming the police: Racial differences in public support for change. *Criminology, 42,* 391-416.

Weitzer, R., & Tuch, S. A. (2005). Racially biased policing: Determinants of citizen perceptions. *Social Forces, 83,* 1,009-1,030.

Withrow, B. L. (2006). *Racial profiling: From rhetoric to reason.* Upper Saddle River, NJ: Prentice Hall.

Selling Savage Portrayals

Young Black and Latino Males in the Carceral State

Natalie Byfield

Fanning the Flames

As the Central Park jogger story unfolded, policy makers, academics, and other researchers from across the city and the nation weighed in on the significance of the attack and offered explanations and potential remedies for violence in the streets. Their solutions often leaned in the direction of more punitive law enforcement methods, as opposed to increasing social programs, banning weapons, or instituting other preventative measures. Nearly a month after the jogger was raped, on May 15, 1989, President George H. W. Bush announced a $1.2 billion anticrime spending package. In his statement announcing the plan, the president mentioned the rape of the jogger in Central Park, along with the murder of Michael Griffith in Howard Beach.[1] His plan called for the bulk of the allocation, $1 billion, to be spent on building new federal prisons (Weinraub 1989).

The focus on punitive as opposed to preventative measures could hardly have been a shock for New Yorkers. Their state was one of the first to rely on the adult criminal justice system to address the problem of juvenile crime. In 1978, New York state strengthened its juvenile offender law to incorporate violent juveniles into the adult court system. And across the nation a few states followed suit. But in the wake of the attack on the jogger, policy makers renewed their efforts to incorporate juveniles into the adult criminal justice system. Included in the public policy response to the rape was a sea change in the ways in which the majority of U.S. states addressed juveniles who committed violent crimes. Forty-four states across the nation began to embrace juveniles within the jurisdiction of the adult criminal courts. The new juvenile justice laws had their greatest impact on the lives of black and Latino youths. In the wake of the jogger incident the discourse from elected leadership, officials in the criminal justice system, and the media stoked fears around the issue of crime and the associations among race, crime, and youth. As a result of the ensuing moral panic, communities across the nation reshaped themselves.

Moral Panic, Wilding, and the War on Drugs

With the jogger case, the media introduced "wilding" into the public discourse as a new, depraved phenomenon in the ever-growing and increasingly heinous inventory of violent acts committed by young people. The New York City media appeared to be creating an association between acts of wilding and black and Latino youths. Moving forward after the rape of the Central Park jogger, the term "wilding" was reserved particularly for references to crimes committed by young blacks and Latinos (Welch, Price, and Yankey 2002, 2004).

The media construction of the wilding phenomenon as a part of the jogger incident allowed the case to have a greater significance for society than the traditional earlier associations of race and crime (Welch, Price, and Yankey 2002, 2004). "The term wilding made a greater impact on the culture by becoming another synonym for youth violence, contributing to fear of crime and moral panic" (Welch, Price, and Yankey 2002: 7). In this particular case, these researchers argue, the wilding incident caused a moral panic. But, [...] juvenile crime and violence had been viewed in some sectors of the mainstream through a less hysterical lens up until the 1970s (Chang 2005). The circumstances surrounding the rape of the Central Park jogger were positioned far differently. While Welch and colleagues (2002) contend that the jogger incident facilitated a moral panic, I believe that the panic was already under way in U.S. society. While largely ignoring illegal drug use in white and affluent communities, law enforcement centered its attention instead on illegal drug use and the associated violence in minority urban communities; black and Latino youths became the focus of the panic. [Previously], I outlined a number of New York City newspaper stories that conveyed mainstream concern that the drug problem in the United States arose from black and Latino communities and posed a societywide threat as it reached into the "silk-stocking" districts. The occurrence of the attack on the jogger during this period of heightened societal antagonism against young black and Latino males may have contributed to the level of sensationalism in the coverage of the case and the ease with which prosecutors drew the delusional conclusions they did. The jogger case is just another example of how a phenomenon exaggerated during a moral panic not only distorts the immediate reality but has the potential to transform future society in ways that suit the interests of the ruling groups that instigated the panic.

The notion of a moral panic is based on the work of Stanley Cohen (2002), who argues that individuals, groups, or events can sometimes be defined as a momentous threat to society and singled out for action. Through a commingling of interests, the media, clergy, elected officials, and criminal justice officials exaggerate the threat and use their resources to come up with self-serving solutions. Cohen's concept of moral panic (as expressed in his *Folk Devils and Moral Panics,* first published in 1972) was the basis of work by Stuart Hall et al. (1978) that examined the so-called problem of muggings in England in the 1970s. Hall et al. (1978) found that reports in the British press about the crisis related to this "new" phenomenon called "muggings" were really just exaggerated claims "factualized" in the media with the help of elected officials and the criminal justice system. Hall et al. (1978) concluded that these groups together set off the moral panic around the muggings. The moral panic represented a crisis in hegemony within the British state. They found that this crisis was, in part, created by changing attitudes among young immigrants, primarily black Caribbeans, who unlike their parents were not political accommodationists and were growing increasingly disenfranchised as an economic recession took hold and they became the targets of racist policies (Hall et al. 1978: 348–355).

In the United States in the 1980s, the moral panic around illegal drug use and the concomitant violence that goes along with the drug trade had already begun to single out young black and Latino males among the group targeted for extraordinary punishment by the state. This moral panic had the earmarks of a contemporary racial project for its potential to reorganize the society's relationship to blacks and Latinos. The type of marginalization experienced by young black and Latino males is tantamount to permanently kicking them out of or keeping them out of the "system," that is, denying them any type of access to mainstream life. Researchers have found a relationship among the nation's transition to a service economy from a manufacturing economy, high rates of unemployment for members of racially marginalized urban groups, and participation in the drug trade by members of these groups (Alexander 2010: 50; Bourgois 1995). While the economy was undergoing this structural transformation, federal, state, and local governments were also changing their criminal justice policies and policing practices to fight crime, specifically launching the so-called War on Drugs. Once they have been incarcerated, these young men have slim chance of finding regular gainful employment upon release.

Michelle Alexander (2010) argues that the War on Drugs was born out of a political response forged by conservative ruling elites threatened by African American demands for equality. This response began in the 1960s civil rights era as a backlash against the seeming social, economic, and political gains being made by African Americans (Alexander 2010). Crime became the rallying cry of right-wing and conservative politicians on their long march back from Barry Goldwater's 1964 Republican Party, as they sought to regain power and control over the social and political agendas of the United States (Pager 2007). The conjoining of the civil rights, black power, and middle-class (largely white) antiwar movements in the mid- to late 1960s so concerned those in power, primarily the political conservatives, that federal and state systems responded with a moral crusade implemented through stricter anticrime measures (Murch 2010; see also Pager 2007).[2] The Nixon administration, which came to power in 1969, gave birth to the Omnibus Crime Control Act in the early 1970s and initiated the War on Crime. Anticrime measures were so much a feature of the identity of the Republican Party that members of even the liberal wing of the party joined the anticrime crusade (Pager 2010). Governor Nelson Rockefeller of New York instituted the Rockefeller drug laws in the early 1970s, which imposed mandatory sentencing for even low-level drug dealers and drug addicts at the street level. These draconian measures disproportionately punished blacks and Latinos.

The conservative movement of the 1960s and 1970s blossomed into the Reagan administration, whose drug war policies instituted in the early 1980s became the most important piece of a "moral crusade" against the upheavals of the 1960s. The law-and-order, anticrime agenda at the federal level was supposed to return moral order to the nation (Alexander 2010; Pager 2007). This new conservative political movement interpreted the social and political agenda associated with liberal programs like the War on Poverty as "permissive" and sought to frame society's conflicts over the appropriate socioeconomic and political path forward as a "problem of moral order" (Pager 2007: 17). The War on Crime, which began in the Nixon administration, would continue through subsequent administrations, each with its own focus and each incorporating more punitive means to address what was defined as the nation's crime problem. Reagan brought the crime-fighting focus to drugs, and in the mid-1980s, with the introduction of crack cocaine into the cornucopia of illegal drugs already used in the United States, the nation experienced dramatic changes in patterns of incarceration. Crack cocaine's marketability—given its relatively low cost—to poor urban kids, and the participation of the unemployed urban poor in the sale of crack through low-level street hustling, allowed for an association among drug use, drug-related crimes, and race. This association was seen as particularly strong in a relatively insulated arena of illegal drug activities in the United States—the segregated, isolated black and Latino "margins" in urban areas. But, due to the ongoing moral panic over crime and drug abuse, an association among youth, drug crimes, and race became defined as a societywide problem, with black and Latino youths demonized as the new folk devils (Reinarman and Le-vine 2006). This allowed the mainstream media to more fully participate in a racial project that began with the political right's attempt to reimpose the moral order.

Symbols in Defense of the New Political Economy

After the introduction of crack cocaine into the illegal drug markets of the United States, the media became an important site for the government's advance campaigns in the War on Drugs

(Alexander 2010: 50–51; Reinarman and Levine 2006). Alexander noted:

> The Reagan administration leaped at the opportunity to publicize crack cocaine in inner-city communities in order to build support for its new war.
>
> In October 1985, the DEA sent Robert Stutman[3] to serve as director of its New York City office and charged him with the responsibility of shoring up public support for the administration's new war. Stutman developed a strategy for improving relations with the news media and sought to draw journalists' attention to the spread of crack cocaine. (2010: 51)

The administration of George H. W. Bush launched the first campaign in its War on Drugs in the press. President Bush appointed William Bennett as his "drug czar," the media title for the head of the newly formed Office of National Drug Control Policy. Bennett had held a cabinet post from 1985 to 1988 as President Ronald Reagan's secretary of education, and he developed Bush's contribution to the drug war in a plan called "The National Drug Control Strategy." The plan, which would increase federal antidrug spending, cited crack as the cause of "the intensifying drug-related chaos" in U.S. society (Bennett 1989: 3). In selling this plan to the public, the Bush administration deliberately misrepresented the drug problem in the Washington, D.C., area. The first salvo came in a speech from the Oval Office:

> On September 5, 1989, President Bush, speaking from the presidential desk in the Oval Office, announced his plan for achieving "victory over drugs" in his first major prime-time address to the nation, broadcast on all three national television networks.... During the address, Bush held up to the cameras a clear plastic bag of crack labeled "EVIDENCE." (Reinarman and Levine (2006: 48)

Bush announced that the evidence had come from Lafayette Park, across the street from the White House, in an attempt to illustrate how overrun the whole society had become by drugs (Bush 1989). However, the drug bust had been set up by Bush officials. The press would later expose the lengths the Bush administration officials had gone through to construct the scenario. Citing the September 22, 1989, *Washington Post* story written by Michael Isikoff, Reinarman and Levine wrote:

> White House Communications Director David Demar[e]st asked Cabinet Affairs Secretary David Bates to instruct the Justice Department "to find some crack that fit the description in the speech." Bates called Richard Weatherbee, special assistant to Attorney General Dick Thornburgh, who then called James Mil[l]ford, executive assistant to the DEA chief. Finally, Mil[l]ford phoned William McMull[a]n, special agent in charge of the DEA's Washington office, and told him to arrange an undercover crack buy near the White House because "evidently, the President wants to show it could be bought anywhere" (Isikoff, 1989).
>
> Despite their best efforts, the top federal drug agents were not able to find anyone selling crack (or any other drug) in Lafayette Park, or anywhere else in the vicinity of the White House. Therefore, in order to carry out their assignment, DEA agents had to entice someone to come to the park to make the sale. Apparently, the only person the DEA could convince was Keith Jackson, an eighteen-year-old African-American high school senior ... (Isikoff, 1989). (Reinarman and Levine 2006: 49)

Revelations about these obvious attempts at public deception did not deter the Bush administration from its course in the drug war. Bennett planned to solve the nation's drug problems by pumping disproportionately larger amount of funds into law enforcement as opposed to treatment (Berke 1989). According to a 2007 report analyzing twenty-five years of the War on Drugs produced by the Sentencing Project, a nonprofit advocacy group focused on criminal justice policy issues, "Drug arrests have more than tripled in the last 25 years, totaling a record 1.8 million arrests in 2005" (Mauer and King 2007: 2). Law enforcement methods targeted street level dealers and the users of crack cocaine rather than users of powder cocaine (Alexander 2010; Reinarman and Levine 2006). "Drug offenders in prisons and jails have increased 1100% since 1980. Nearly a half-million (493,800) persons are in state or federal prison or local jail for a drug offense, compared to an estimated 41,100 in 1980" (Mauer and King 2007: 2).

This strategy incarcerated disproportionately large numbers of blacks and Latinos, who filled the ranks of street level dealers and who were predominantly users of crack cocaine, as compared to whites, who typically abused powder cocaine (Reinarman and Levine 2006). While African Americans made up 14 percent of regular drug users, non-Hispanic whites 69.2 percent, and Hispanics 12.4 percent, "African Americans are 37% of those arrested for drug offenses and 56% of persons in state prison for drug offenses," according to the Sentencing Project report (Mauer and King 2007: 19–20). Media coverage of these law enforcement practices often ignored the racial disparities in the treatment of black and white offenders within the criminal justice system, reinforcing in the public discourse the association between black race and crime, particularly violent crime, and further advancing this association as some type of race-based biological imperative for crime and violence (Reinarman and Levine 2006).[4]

The news media were an important site for reconstructing the definition of black and Latino male youth as the War on Drugs got under way. The rape of the Central Park jogger in the midst of all this only amplified the existing state of moral panic. As it was represented in the media, the case heightened in the public's mind the type of threat that young black and Latino males represented in society. In my content analysis of the Central Park jogger press reports, I examined the features of an individual's social location that played a major role in the coverage—features of race, class, victimhood, gender, and age.[5] Here I highlight how the press reports of the jogger incident defined the suspects and the jogger in relation to each other.

While indicators for race were dominant in the press reports, indicators for class were the features of individual identities most often used to mark membership within categorical groupings. This made class

the concept that appeared most frequently to readers.[6] Ninety-eight percent of the articles had at least one indicator for class [...]. In my study, three class indicators represented identity: runner, jogger, and avid runner. Nine class indicators represented institutions: jogger's universities, jogger's family and friends' universities, jogger's family and friends' jobs, jogger's non-Salomon job, Salomon Brothers, investment banker, schools suspects attended, suspects' family and friends' schools, and suspects' family and friends' jobs. Three class indicators represented social structure: jogger middle class, suspects' moderate income, and suspects' middle-class lifestyles. [...]

From a sociological point of view, most of the indicators of class used in the jogger coverage were based on institutions. Thus, the meaning that the concept of class took on in the coverage was largely as an important societal institution. Given this link in the press reports, it is possible that the coverage left audiences with the impression that the attack on the jogger represented an attack on important institutions. The jogger worked for the now-defunct investment bank Salomon Brothers, one of the powerhouses of the Wall Street community at the time, which was central to the new symbolic economic order [...]. This new economic system had shrugged off the manufacturing jobs that had at one time sustained the people in the margins. In their content analysis of the jogger coverage, which was organized differently from mine, Welch, Price, and Yankey came to a similar conclusion: "The rape of the 'young Manhattan investment banker' seems to represent a symbolic attack on the political economy by the so-called dangerous class" (2002: 21).

In the context of the press reports on the jogger's rape, the concept of gender was largely based on issues of identity. Seven of the ten indicators for gender were words related to gender identity: female, woman, pretty, attractive, bubbly, she/her, and breast. Three of the indicators for gender were based on violent social acts that subordinate: rape, sodomy, and gang-rape. The two most frequently used indicators for gender were "rape," which appeared in 84 percent of the articles, and "woman," which was included in 53 percent of the articles. [...] Like race, gender is an aspect of identity. And, as in the case of racial identity, gender identity is constructed, in part, through interactions in the social world. As a subordinating act, rape gives gender its meaning. In the context of the jogger coverage, the suspects' race is privileged over gender oppression/subordination as a feature of the coverage. In the analysis, the "black and Latino" race of the suspects cannot be separated from the act of rape.[7] Thus, the term "rape" also becomes associated with race, either the jogger's or the suspects'.

However, the concept of gender did not appear to dominate the coverage in a story purportedly about a rape incident. The jogger was a raped woman and as such her identity was marked by this vulnerability, which the media treated as something that warranted protection. Media organizations, in general, including those incorporated in my study, withheld publication of the jogger's name to protect her privacy. This is common practice when reporting cases of rape. However, the *Amsterdam News,* a Harlem-based black-owned and -run newspaper, published the jogger's name, to much criticism from the mainstream press. Journalist Timothy Sullivan (1992) noted in his book about the case that the *Amsterdam News* named the jogger because mainstream papers had identified the black and Latino underage suspects by name and address, a deviation from common practice concerning young people accused of committing crimes.

The significant point here is that the media appeared to use some type of hierarchy to determine who in the jogger case warranted protection. While it initially appeared that the issue of protection revolved around the identity category "raped woman," there may have been other factors operating. The person who was raped did not become known to the public as a "raped woman"; she became known as the "jogger." Additionally, other women who were raped around that time were not brought significantly into the coverage of the Central Park incident. In the context of my study,

the term "jogger" is one of the indicators of class. In the coverage, it was the most frequently used indicator of class, appearing in 95 percent of all the articles in the sample and in 99 percent of all the stories in Time Periods 3 and 4 (the post-trial coverage). [...]

Kristin Bumiller (2008) argues that the jogger became an iconic symbol within the movement against sexual violence, but she was a different type of symbol for the mainstream press. My content analysis suggests that, within the media, the jogger was not an iconic representation of crimes against women, because the rape culture in U.S. society was not an element of the coverage. Although the media had the opportunity to associate the attack with the agenda of the women's movement, they chose to use the jogger to deliver a different message.

The jogger was the iconic representation of an attack against an important societal and economic institution. Male-dominated corporate America, the physical representation of capitalism, was being symbolically projected in the mainstream media as vulnerable to disruption, and low-income, young black males were presented as the biggest threat to the behemoth system undergirding corporate America. While class and gender references constituted the most frequently used language in the jogger coverage, in the era of color blindness class and gender as concepts were used to mask a racist attack against young black males. Black male sexuality has historically been a symbol of danger in U.S. society, and it has typically been presented as a danger specifically to white women. Near the end of the twentieth century, as the mainstream grew more inclusive, however, those managing the mainstream boundaries appeared to be ensuring that black masculinity would be limited in mainstream spaces.

"Science" Reshapes the Society

This would not be the first time black males were represented as a threat to society. There is a long history in U.S. culture, from the days of early America, of constructing associations between the black or nonwhite "race" and savagery (Fredrickson 1971a) and doing so

with the help of "science" (Banton 2009; Jordan 1968). This new moral crusade also received its imprimatur from academia.[8] Theories about a black subculture of violence had developed from the late 1960s, when the moral crusade began (Wolfgang 1983; Wolfgang and

Ferracuti 1967), and this work was used by others to develop newer theories about the propensity for violence among low-income urban black males.

The message in the media coverage of the jogger case, coming amidst the trend of rising youth violence, seemed to take hold of the imaginations of important members of the academic and governmental elites. Some in academic circles returned to "scientific analysis" to further develop the 1960s conceptualizations of black and Latino youths as innately violent. In the late 1980s, the research of political scientist John J. DiIulio Jr. (1989: 35) blamed the dismal life conditions of poor people of color in urban areas on "the large numbers of chronic and predatory street criminals." By 1995, he had constructed his notion of the "super-predator," a category of juvenile criminals who supposedly would be more deadly than anything witnessed before in the United States (DiIulio 1995).[9] DiIulio (1995) based his conclusions on (1) old birth-cohort studies of 10,000 Philadelphia boys born in 1945 (Wolfgang 1983)[10] and (2) research by contemporary criminologists that extrapolated from the birth-cohort studies to predict the number of juvenile offenders in the future (J. Q. Wilson 1995). DiIulio stated that of the boys between ten and eighteen years old in the birth-cohort studies, "more than one-third had at least one recorded arrest by the time they were 18" (1995: 31). He also noted that "two-thirds of all the violent crimes committed by the cohort" were committed by about 6 percent of the boys (DiIulio 1995: 31). The findings of the birth-cohort study, along with projections of an unchanging rate of delinquency led DiIulio to concur with predictions by James Q. Wilson and other criminologists that, given the birth rates of the time, an "additional 500,000 boys who will be 14 to 17 years old in the year 2000 will mean at least 30,000 more murderers, rapists and muggers on the streets than we have today" (DiIulio 1995: 31).

DiIulio (1995) predicted that this newly expanded group of "super-predators" would be much more dangerous than earlier groups because they were being raised in a state of moral poverty, which he defined as follows:

[It] is the poverty of being without loving, capable, responsible adults who teach you right from wrong. It is the poverty of being without parents and other authorities who habituate you to feel joy at others' joy, pain at others' pain, happiness when you do right, remorse when you do wrong. It is the poverty of growing up in the virtual absence of people who teach morality by their own everyday example and who insist that you follow suit.

In the extreme, moral poverty is the poverty of growing up surrounded by deviant, delinquent, and criminal adults in abusive, violence-ridden, fatherless, Godless and jobless settings. In sum, whatever their material circumstances, kids of whatever race, creed or color are most likely to become criminally depraved when they are morally deprived....

The abject moral poverty that creates super-predators begins very early in life in homes where unconditional love is nowhere but unmerciful abuse is common. (DiIulio 1995: 31)

The message here was clear: The rising rate of youth violence was unavoidable and our society had better be prepared for it. The youth who were primarily targeted in DiIulio's (1995) declaration were black and Latino young males living in urban areas.

At the nexus of research and public policy, DiIulio's work was quite influential. He wrote, along with William Bennett and John P. Walters, *Body Count: Moral Poverty ... And How to Win America's War against Crime and Drugs,* about the centrality of drug abuse to crime (Bennett, DiIulio, and Walters 1996). Given his access to high-level policy makers (including testimony before Congress) and the national media attention his ideas received in *Time* and *Newsweek* (Annin 1996; Zoglin, Allis, and Kamlani 1996), it is no surprise that DiIulio's work also had a dramatic effect on policies affecting juveniles (Keenan 2005). This work shaped policy by way of contributing to state and federal authorities' reliance on incarceration as a means of addressing crime (Pager 2007). Years later, DiIulio would recant his theory of the rise of the "super-predator" (Becker 2001), but that came after it had already buttressed the transformation of juvenile justice laws, supporting the use of more extreme law enforcement methods—including imprisonment in adult facilities—for young offenders (Hancock 2003; Keenan 2005). In 2012,

DiIulio went so far as to join in a friend of the court brief filed with the U.S. Supreme Court in two cases involving harsh sentencing of juveniles.[11] The brief argued, in part, that the "super-predator" theory had no validity.

Although DiIulio had been renouncing his own theory publicly since 2001 (Becker 2001), as recently as 2005, his colleague William Bennett continued to promulgate biological correlations between race and crime. While in conversation with a caller to his syndicated radio talk show, Bennett offered a "hypothetical proposition" for reducing crime—"Abort every black baby" in the country—then immediately countered that this solution to crime was "morally reprehensible" (CNN 2005). Underlying Bennett's comment, however, is the assertion that there is likely a biological association between race and crime.

Society's response to the growing drug problem in the United States was to construct associations between race and crime. These associations have become much more salient because research that draws connections among race, crime, and youth has been given a great deal of attention in the media. Media language has used such connections to essentially form a symbolic framework that allows for the reification of associations among race, crime, and youth.

Reifying Racial Meaning in the Criminal Justice System

The moral panic in which the Central Park jogger's rape was enveloped had already embraced increased rates of incarceration as a solution to the problems of crime in general and drug crimes in particular. The sensationalized coverage of the rape exacerbated this approach; as some juvenile justice advocates noted (Ryan and Ziedenberg 2007), it intensified the panic, leading to a transformation in the juvenile justice system.[12] Of the six young suspects charged with the jogger's rape, five were tried in adult court (the sixth entered a plea bargain), but five were sentenced as juveniles. In my content analysis of the press reports during Time Period 2, the legal phase of the coverage, one of the most curious findings was the sharply diminished use of words or terms that served as racial indicators[...]. In Time Period 1, during the construction of the narrative, 67 percent of the articles included at least one indicator for race. This was a relatively low frequency of use for racial indicators, considering that so many perceived the case to be about race. Even more surprisingly, however, during the second time period (the legal phase), the proportion of articles with at least one racial indicator fell to 49 percent. This was a decrease of 18 percentage points in the use of indicators of racial categorical groupings. (See Table 1.4.1) What could account for such a steep decline?

It appears that, for media content producers, when the legal system was part of the subject of press reports, representations of black and Latino racial groupings[13] were less important as an explicit feature of the coverage. This may have been the case because race, particularly black racial identity, was becoming much more associated with the criminal justice system. New anticrime measures had vastly increased the rate of incarceration in the United States for all people (Mauer and King 2007: 2; Pager 2007), but incarceration of African Americans was disproportionately high relative to their rate of arrest (Mauer and King 2007: 2; Pager 2007; Wacquant 2002). This disparity

TABLE 1.4.1 **Percentages of Articles that Included at Least One Indicator for Each of the Major Concepts of Coverage, by Time Period**

Concept	Time Period 1: Apr 21, 1989–Jun 9, 1989	Time Period 2: Jun 10, 1989–Mar 14, 1991	Time Periods 3 and 4: Mar 15, 1991–Dec 31, 2003
Race	67.3	49.2	78.9
Violence	96.4	92.5	92.1
Class	96.4	96.7	100.0
Gender	98.2	93.2	94.7
Age	89.1	74.2	89.5
Victimhood	63.6	36.7	36.5
Sample size	N = 55	N = 120	N = 76

suggests that the moral panic that drove the War on Drugs had transformed the criminal justice system into a system of mass incarceration for black males, and had so united perceptions of "criminal" and "black race" that the societal meaning assigned to members of this racial group had been transformed. Thus, the War on Drugs greatly exacerbated the marginalization of people in a social location that included black race, lower income, male gender, and conviction for a felony. Sociologists Devah Pager (2007) and Loïc Wacquant (2002) and critical race scholar Michelle Alexander (2010) have come to similar conclusions in recent studies. Wacquant (2002) argues that the increasing levels of incarceration of African Americans have come to represent one of four "peculiar institutions" (the others being slavery, Jim Crow, and the construction of the ghettos) that have confined blacks over the course of U.S. history. Given the way in which the War on Drugs criminalized blacks, and the attendant increase in rates of incarceration of blacks, the black racial grouping became closely associated with people ensnared by the criminal justice system. This close association between "black race" and "subjects in the criminal justice system," which was supported by the results of my content analysis, came shortly after the period in U.S. history when blacks for the first time began to outnumber whites in the national inmate population.[14]

Incorporating Juveniles into the System of Mass Incarceration

By the time the Central Park jogger story broke, public discourse had been primed with these notions of an association—possibly biological but certainly cultural—between race and crime. One of the greatest ironies and injustices of the jogger case is that the six accused teens were in fact innocent. Media sensationalism in the coverage of the story has been blamed for heightening the atmosphere of fear in society. In the wake of the case, there was a ramping up of juvenile justice laws, beginning in the period 1992–1999, in which most states in the United States passed laws designed to try more juveniles as adults (Keenan 2005; Ryan and Ziedenberg 2007).[15] After spiking in the mid-1990s, rates of juvenile crime have declined "for a dozen years to a 30-year low" (Ryan and Ziedenberg 2007: 4).

Following the attack on the jogger and the trials of the defendants, states across the nation expanded the scope of their juvenile justice laws by changing the boundaries of jurisdiction for juvenile courts. Between 1992 and 1997, forty-four states put new laws on the books or expanded existing laws that allowed juveniles to be tried as adults in criminal court, according to a report published by the U.S. Department of Justice, Office of Juvenile Justice and Delinquency Prevention (Snyder and Sickmund 1999). Academics and policy makers at the highest levels of government provided a rationale for these changes through the construction of the now-defunct theory of the "super-predator"

(DiIulio 1995; Krajicek 1999). The jogger case seemed to add to the empirical evidence needed to justify the racial project that right-wing policy makers began in the wake of the social movements of the 1960s. The problem, of course, is that the case against the suspects in the jogger attack itself was constructed; the boys were innocent.

The transformation of the juvenile justice system in the wake of the jogger case has had a disproportionate impact on black and Latino youths in the United States, forever ensnaring them in this nation's system of mass incarceration. According to juvenile justice advocates, approximately 200,000 youths are prosecuted in adult courts annually (Ryan and Ziedenberg 2007). Although many of these minors do not end up in adult prisons, thirty-one states now have laws that require that young people tried once in juvenile court must be tried for subsequent offenses in adult criminal court. These changes in juvenile justice laws suggests a possible impact of media coverage of youth on U.S. social structure. The disproportionate impact on black and Latino youths indicates how media associations of race, youth, and crime have become reified in the social structure.

While juvenile justice advocates are fighting for changes in the system, it is important to note the effectiveness of these laws. The changes have become institutionalized as crime prevention and reduction measures. However, researcher Jeffrey A. Butts (2012) found that there is no relationship between the placement of juveniles in the adult or criminal court system and a reduction in violent crime. He noted:

> At first glance, it may appear that the greater use of transfer lowered violent youth crime, but this argument is refuted by a simple analysis of crime trends. In the six states that allow fair comparisons (i.e., where all juveniles ages 16–19 are originally subject to juvenile court jurisdiction and sufficient data exist for the calculations), the use of criminal court transfer bears no relationship to changes in juvenile violence. (Butts 2012)

States have been increasing prosecutorial power or have created laws that enable them to bypass family court and transfer youthful offenders to criminal court. According to Butts (2012), "entire classes of young offenders are transferred without the involvement of the court."

The reification of associations of race, youth, and crime in the social structure is dialectically related to the mainstream media renditions that normalize the marginalization of black and Latino youths, particularly male youths, from the mainstream. They stand apart, distinct from categorical groupings of other youths, vulnerable but despised.

NOTES

1. Mentioning the attack on the Central Park jogger and the murder Michael Griffith in the same context suggests that even at the federal level there was an attempt to create moral equivalence between the two incidents and to suggest that both were possibly symbolic of the perils of racial border crossings.

2. Hall et al. (1978) also credit a conservative backlash, starting in the 1960s in Great Britain, as part of the reason for that moral panic around muggings.

3. At the time of Robert Stutman's retirement in 1990, a *New York Times* report (Kerr 1990) stated that he was critical of U.S. drug policies because of the meager spending on drug treatment and education.

4. Although the idea of race as a social construction has been the dominant paradigm, biologically based ideas of race still existed and continue to exist. In science, when new paradigms emerge, followers of the old theories often continue to try to prove the worth of the old paradigm. See Kuhn 1962.

5. The findings from my content analysis point to the ways in which media producers conceptualize the world outside their institutional doors.

6. This does not make class the most important concept in the coverage. In the context of media systems, analyses that rely on frequencies will not indicate the degree or level of importance. In media, importance is determined by prominent placement of stories. Therefore, the frequency of inclusion of indicators for the concept of class does not determine how important class was to the media content makers. Krippendorff (2004: 195) notes that in content analyses "simple frequencies say nothing about relationships between content variables." Additional analysis would be needed to determine the relationships between the concepts and prominent placement in media.

7. Interracial rapes are more frequently covered by the media than rapes in which the perpetrator and victim are from the same racial category.

8. See also note 4 above.

9. See also Krajicek 1999 on the history of Dilulio's concept of the "super-predator." Satcher (2001) argues in his study on youth violence that the notion of a "super-predator" is one of the "myths" about young people and violence.

10. Marvin E. Wolfgang's (1983) birth-cohort studies form the basis of all of this work by John J. Dilulio Jr. and James Q. Wilson.

11. In what was essentially a repudiation of their earlier work, Dilulio and several prominent criminologists who had supported the "super-predator" theory joined a 2012 friend of the court brief supporting the petitioners in two cases heard together in which the U.S. Supreme Court would be ruling on the "constitutionality of sentences of life without parole for

juveniles convicted of homicide offenses, including felony homicide" (p. 2). The brief stated that "Empirical research that has analyzed the increase in violent crime … demonstrates that the juvenile superpredator was a myth and the predictions of future youth violence were baseless" (p. 8). See U.S. Supreme Court brief in the cases of petitioners *Kuntrell Jackson v. Ray Hobbs, Director, Arkansas Department of Corrections,* and *Evan Miller v. Alabama,* 10-9647 and 10-9646, amici curiae brief filed by Carl Micarelli, Counsel of Record, January 17, 2012.

12. Ryan and Ziedenberg (2007: 3) directly cite the Central Park jogger case in their report. "Sometimes all it takes is *one case* to change the course of public opinion and national policy. The Central Park Jogger case did just that." Their conclusions are not scientifically drawn, and the organization they produced their study for—Campaign for Youth Justice—is engaged in a national campaign to end youth incarceration in adult facilities across the nation.

13. All but two of the eighteen racial words or terms refer to black and Latino race.

14. Wacquant (2002) argues that mass incarceration operates like slavery as an institution that defines blacks in the United States. He noted that the inmate population in the United States was predominantly white until 1988.

15. See also the U.S. Supreme Court brief cited in note 11 for this chapter.

REFERENCES

Hall, Stuart, Chas Critcher, Tony Jefferson, John Clarke, and Brian Roberts. 1978. *Policing the Crisis: Mugging, the State, and Law and Order.* London: MacMillan.

Kerr, Peter. 1990. "Retiring Agents Sharply Attack Drug Policies." *New York Times,* March 1, p. B1.

Krajicek, David. 1999. "'Super-Predators': The Making of a Myth." *Youth Today* 8 (April): 4.

Krippendorff, Klaus. 2004. *Content Analysis: An Introduction to Its Methodology.* 2nd ed. Thousand Oaks, CA: Sage Publications.

Kuhn, Thomas. 1962. *Structure of Scientific Revolutions.* Chicago: University of Chicago Press.

Ryan, Liz, and Jason Ziedenberg. 2007. "The Consequences Aren't Minor: The Impact of Trying Youth as Adults and Strategies for Reform." *Campaign for Youth Justice Report,* March. Washington, DC: Campaign for Youth Justice. Executive Summary available at http://www.campaign4youthjustice.org/Downloads/NationalReportsArticles/JPI014-Consequences_exec.pdf.

Satcher, David. 2001. *Surgeon General Report.* Washington, DC: U.S. Department of Health and Human Services. Available at http://www.ncbi.nlm.nih.gov/books/NBK44297/#A12312.

Wacquant, Loïc. 2002. "From Slavery to Mass Incarceration: Rethinking the 'Race Question' in the US." *New Left Review* 13 (Jan–Feb): 41–60.

Wolfgang, Marvin E. 1983. "Delinquency in Two Birth Cohorts." *American Behavioral Scientist* 27 (1): 75–86.

PART 2

Policing Latinos

Policing the Anticommunity

Race, Deterritorialization, and Labor Market Reorganization in South Los Angeles

Aaron Roussell

Recent decades have seen the rise of both community partnerships and the carceral state. Community policing in Los Angeles arose after the 1992 uprisings and was built on two conceptual building blocks—the territorial imperative and community partnership—which remain central more than 20 years later. At the same time, LA has undergone a significant black-to-Latino demographic shift linked with its restructured economy. This article discusses these changes using archival analysis and 5 years of participant observation in one South LA precinct. Police help to reshape the demography of South LA in ways conducive to post-Fordist economic shifts. The "community" concept appropriated by urban governance initiatives is composed against an unwanted "anticommunity," which serves to heighten territorial control over black and Latino residents. Rather than encourage community cogovernance over the institution of policing, community rhetoric facilitates racial preference in neighborhood transition under the auspices of an increasingly bifurcated labor market.

The rise of community partnerships in urban governance has increasingly dominated the discussion on crime, law, social services, and institutional initiatives (Brown 2010; Herbert and Brown 2006; Hughes and Edwards 2002; Myers and Goddard 2013; Rose 1996). A parallel trend, referred to by such phrases as the carceral state, the prison nation, and the new social control, has seen the rise of mass incarceration, as well as the increased regulation and surveillance of public space and black and brown populations (Beckett and Herbert 2009; Foucault 1995; Gelman, Fagan, and Kiss 2007; Richie

2012; Stuart 2011). Implicated in both of these currents has been the adoption of community policing by nearly every major urban police force in the country (Johnson and Roth 2003), a tactical and philosophical shift which purports to reconnect urban populations with those agents the state has assigned to protect citizens and maintain order. Focusing on the shifting demographic and economic terrain of Los Angeles, this article describes ways in which community policing helps remake urban neighborhoods. The community in community policing, rather than reflecting organic notions of residents, conforms to police notions of territorial control.

The Los Angeles Police Department (LAPD) began implementing community policing in 1992, in tandem with the national push for such initiatives. This effort was not a spontaneous desire to engage more closely with LA residents, but rather a political response to the 1991 police beating of motorist Rodney King and the 1992 uprisings that followed the acquittal of his assailants by a white jury in Ventura County. Residents, particularly in majority black and Latino South LA where the uprisings began, exerted collective pressure to combat police racism and brutality (Costa Vargas 2006; Davis 1993a; Loyd 2012). The independent Christopher Commission Report generated in the interim recommended community policing as one way to make police "accountable to all segments of the community" and create a more "positive relationship" with the community (1991: 105–106). The LAPD's resulting community policing approach remains the official response to calls for police accountability in LA.

Although the popular image of South Los Angeles is that of an African-American ghetto—a "spatially segregated and contiguous Black community" (Patillo 2003: 1046)—black residence began to decline in the early 1980s from a height of about 85 percent. By 2007, South LA was over half Latino and nearly one-third immigrant, a number which certainly undercounts the undocumented population (Hipp et al. 2010). Families with sufficient means of all ethnoracial groups have left South LA for the LA Harbor, Long Beach, and the suburbs (Davis 1993b; Soja 2014). As Costa Vargas (2006) suggests, South LA "is quickly becoming the exclusive home of the brown and black California version of the *lumpenproletariat*, and as such has become the site for an unprecedented volume of imprisonment and deaths" (28)—a broad statement supported by other LA researchers (Davis 2006; Stuart 2011; Valle and Torres 2000). Linking demographic transition to urban governance, Costa Vargas suggests that up to 14 percent of black outmigration from LA in the 1980s and 1990s was due solely to the forced "migration" of incarceration.

These demographic shifts are also linked to the vast urban restructuring that LA has undergone since the 1970s (Soja 2014; Soja, Morales, and Wolff 1983). The rise of LA's bifurcated service and information economy in place of its postwar manufacturing dominance has provided the area with limited job growth, swelling the Latino population of South LA by pulling immigrants from Mexico and Central America (Ibarra and Carlos 2015; Valle and Torres 2000). Such a post-Fordist arrangement allows for both investment in high status, high income technology and entertainment industries on the one hand and a supportive economy of workers carrying out low-status, labor-intensive tasks on the other. By the end of the 1990s, LA remained the largest industrial city in the United States, but its "industries [were] based on nonunionized low-wage workers … drawn increasingly from the ranks of immigrants, legal and undocumented" (Valle and Torres 2000: 4). Many service employers, such as hotels and cleaning services, explicitly prefer immigrant and undocumented Latinos over native-born black citizens. One ostensible reason for this is their "soft skills": Zamudio and Lichter (2008) argue that this is code for tractable immigrant labor, as undocumented migrants can be paid substandard wages, collect no benefits or worker's compensation, and are unlikely to sue over workplace violations. Yet the preference against black labor has long been a historical trend in LA (Sides 2003). As Marcelli, Pastor, and Jossart (1999) remind us, this economic arrangement also swells the ranks of the informal economy of both visible and invisible, citizen and noncitizen labor, including day labor, prostitution, street food vending, and drug selling. Meanwhile, the homeless population has expanded significantly in LA's "Skid Row," about three-fourths of whom are black, particularly since the 2008 housing market crash (Stuart 2011).

To expand on the relationship between the turn to community on the one hand and the growing prison nation on the other, this article situates both trends within a framework that emphasizes the responsivity of each to the racial/capitalist state. It contributes to a developing, place-based literature that considers together political economy, law enforcement, and the racialized social forces that shape urban space. For example, Lynch and her colleagues (2013) identified economic and political pressures from gentrification and tourism as driving differential drug law enforcement in San Francisco. These policies subjected black residents in different neighborhoods to coercive containment or expulsion depending on the political/economic development goals for each neighborhood. In LA, Stuart (2011) finds that special law enforcement task forces sweep homeless populations in "Skid Row" into sub-poverty positions using initiatives underwritten by businesses that profit from this labor. He discusses in other work the rehabilitation-oriented policing of the homeless in Skid Row compared to their expulsion from "prime" commodified urban spaces (Stuart 2014). These authors explicitly connect patterns of racialized law enforcement to neoliberal economic policy, yet such logics are not simply economic, using cultural understandings of racial inferiority to enable policies that would not pass muster if the affected population was white (Alexander 2010; Katznelson 2006).

Germane to this community-governmentality nexus, Brown (2010) considers the failure of federal community-building initiatives in Seattle. She charts the irreconcilable views of those who envisioned community improvement as an enhancement of law enforcement and black residents who insisted on investing in the community's residents directly and policing the police. Also in Seattle, Herbert (2005) suggests that community policing devolves responsibility from the state to local residents. He finds that residents involved in these community-government efforts resent the offloading of government responsibility.

These studies contend that urban police practices implicate a larger consideration of neoliberal governance (Yarwood 2007). Rather than addressing police tactics or backgrounding police as automatons enforcing unjust law, this article extends these analyses by highlighting the dynamic role of police in reshaping urban environments.

The Los Angeles Police Department in South LA provides a case study through which to examine community policing as a political project located at the intersection of these trends. This article argues that police are helping to reshape the demography of urban territory in ways that are conducive to post-Fordist economic shifts. The document analysis and ethnographic methods brought to bear here trace the contours of the LAPD's community concept as one particular mechanism through which this occurs. "Community," in this incarnation, is composed in opposition to an "anticommunity" animated by racial preference and labor utility. The category of anticommunity is instrumental, providing the means to punish and exclude South LA's black community while controlling the influx of Latinos as low-wage and informal labor.

I expand below on the multiple methods used to investigate these concerns and then present the data and analysis over two sections. The first section comprises an analysis of more than two decades of LA's community policing efforts, examining the LAPD vision for community directly. The second section illustrates how the LAPD has operationalized its definitions of community, territory, and partnership to tighten coercive and regulatory control over its impoverished and working class racial geography. These sections build toward a final discussion where these threads draw together into a larger discussion of race, class, territorial policing, and the use of community by the neoliberal state.

Methods

Exploring both the roots and the contemporary fruit of community policing over multiple decades requires multiple methods and data sources. First, archival documents generated by LA municipal government beginning in 1991 provide much of the historical context.[1] These documents outline the collective thought processes that went into the creation of the program. Several are large, well-defined plans

---

1 Special thanks to Cheryl Maxson at the University of California, Irvine, for providing many of these documents from her studies of community policing in LA in the 1990s.

for community policing, exchanged between LA's Commission for Public Safety, City Council, and Police Department, while others are Departmental memoranda intended for officers of all ranks to read, understand, and incorporate into practice. Yet others comprise official and independent assessments of the LAPD after scandals and uprisings. Together they describe the plans for incorporating residents and other stakeholders into the community policing process. They also provide a window into the meanings that the LAPD ascribes to the concept of community—as well as its places of silence (see Smith 2005).

The second portion of this article analyzes LA's contemporary community policing approach. This analysis is drawn from ethnographic data collected over 5 years (beginning in August 2008 and ending in May 2013) in the LAPD precinct referred to pseudonymously as "South Division." The hundreds of hours of participant observation undertaken in South Division mainly comprised attendance at community-police meetings, neighborhood events with a strong police presence, and ridealongs with community policing officers (Senior Lead Officers, or "SLOs"). These investigations also produced more than 50 interviews with residents, neighborhood stakeholders, officers, and police administrators. South Division's SLOs are divided evenly between black, white, and Latino, but I was able to negotiate ridealongs only with the majority Latino and white SLOs during my fieldwork, although I was able to observe them all in other ways. Latino and white SLOs get along well and support each other's efforts, but undermine the integrity and work ethic of the Division's black SLOs behind their backs. As a white man co-conducting research with a Latino partner, I was quickly associated with this dynamic, and consequently was unable to access those networks. Such an addition would deepen the analysis and must be left for future work, but the larger dynamics are unmistakable.

During these sessions, I always carried a notebook and jotted down as much as I could about the scene unfolding before me. Meetings and ridealongs were ideal situations in which to take detailed notes, enabling the recording of entire conversations with key words, phrases, and exchanges largely intact. As soon as possible after these events, I wrote up these jottings into organized sets of fieldnotes, reconstructing observation sessions and situating them with respect to prior events and my own reactions (Atkinson 2001). An hour of observation was equivalent to five or six single spaced pages, and I reproduce some of these below. All names of people, places, and locations are pseudonyms (excluding political figures). All data were entered into MaxQDA qualitative data analysis software for sorting and coding. I used an open coding procedure, noting and memoing while conducting close readings of each piece of text. Themes and subthemes emerged and cohered into the sets of ideas presented here in dialogue with larger theoretical understandings (Emerson 2001; Emerson, Fretz, and Shaw 1995).

Partnership and the Territorial Community: Policing in the 1990s

Definitions of community policing tend to cohere around four major themes (e.g., Goldstein 1987; Skogan and Hartnett 1997; Skolnick and Bayley 1988). First is community crime prevention, which necessitates a public, visible police presence that must be seen as accessible and caring. Second, police patrol must reorient to enhance nonemergency service to render police available and unremarkable. Third is the idea that police must be accountable to the public, engaging not only with supportive residents but also those residents who may level negative feedback. Skolnick and Bayley (1988) suggest that "getting to know people will not work if police insist on one-way communication. Unless police are willing, at the very least, to tolerate public feedback, community policing will be perceived as public relations, and the chasm between police and public will grow wider once again." (10) Finally, police command structure must decentralize to become more adaptable and idiosyncratic to the constituent area. The promises of accountability and partnership in particular make community policing attractive to municipalities undergoing spikes in unrest and dissatisfaction with police (Independent Commission on the Los Angeles Police Department 1991; Johnson and Roth 2003).

Los Angeles' community policing approach remains the ongoing governmental response to calls for police accountability. It has weathered the tempests of the Rampart Scandal (1998–2000), May Day protests (2007), Occupy LA (2010), and ex-LAPD officer Chris Dorner's private war with law enforcement (2013), to name a few. Police presented as governing crime, disorder, and public safety in a different way than they had in the past; a way more in tune with community needs and desires. To effect this, the LAPD had to answer the questions "What is community?" and "What is community's place within police governance?" Rather than tapping indigenous notions of community in ways relevant to the uprisings (Costa Vargas 2006; Loyd 2012), the Department opted to reanimate discarded partnership strategies and reassert control of the city through a rigid territoriality. This section first describes how the LAPD arrogated to itself the task of defining community, and proceeded to position geographic compartmentalization and sociobiological theories of conflict, predation, and ownership as the cornerstone of its community project. It continues by demonstrating how police defined the partnership relationship as community information harvesting and perception management.

THE TERRITORIAL IMPERATIVE

The LAPD has always seen itself as understaffed and outnumbered, using heightened aggression to make up for its perceived manpower deficiencies (Greene 2000; Herbert 1997). Police administrators adopted the "territorial imperative" to remedy this problem in the early 1970s (Los Angeles Police Department 1992, 1999; Parks 1999; Williams 1995). According to LA's Community Policing Implementation Plan (1997): "[Officers will emphasize] the 'territorial imperative,' where police officers and the people they serve take ownership of a Basic Car Area bringing them closer together. This is a key ingredient of Community Policing." The territorial imperative was de-emphasized

in the 1980s, but returned with the 1992 community policing mandate.

In 1966, amateur anthropologist Robert Ardrey published *The Territorial Imperative*, an influential book among social Darwinists. Ardrey described humans and other animals as genetically encoded for territorial dominance, impelling them to violent conflict over geography. Applying crude evolutionary biological reasoning, he argued that if territorial conflict is biologically predetermined, there is little use in attempting to rein in this impulse—instead, better to win and control the territory. In the world of human geography, this reasoning naturalizes oppression as a necessary feature of the contemporary race and class order.[2] After its publication, the LAPD adopted the territorial imperative as organizational ideology, predating the contemporary community policing movement by several decades. As former LAPD administrator Jeff O'Malley suggests in his interview:

> If you want [officers] to become proactive and you want them to take ownership then you have to give them a piece of real estate. That's when the territorial imperative came in. Today I believe, firmly believe, in that if people have ownership, they treat it differently than they would if they don't.

The technology behind the LAPD's territorial imperative is that of division and enumeration. Community, consequently, is overlaid onto a grid designed for territorial control. In the eyes of police, LA comprises increasingly granulated and hierarchical levels of space, beginning with "reporting districts" used for fixing crime locations, aggregating up to "Basic Car Areas" (BCAs; e.g., "18SLO029"), which aggregate again to precincts run by Captains (known as Policing Areas or Divisions), and again to LA's four Bureaus, each headed by a Deputy Chief. In explaining the territorial imperative, one 1990s-era LAPD administrator discussed the Senior Lead Officers (SLOs) in charge of BCAs as "lone predators," in their responsibility

---

2 See Alland (2004) and Lewontin, Rose, and Kamin (1984) for a more nuanced critique of sociobiology generally and the territorial imperative specifically.

to their "real estate." Another used the metaphor of "mountain lions" jealously patrolling their turf and disallowing other officers from jurisdiction except in moments of crisis. Community policing fortified rather than challenged the LAPD's geographic formulation of its mission, drawing its concern for community directly from the territorial imperative.

The LAPD reinforced this geographic interpretation of community by using crime and U.S. census data to conduct a territorial analysis in 1997 through "work load, demographics, natural boundaries, and the identified natural service communities" (Los Angeles Police Department 1992, 1997). This analysis "result[ed] in the creation of an additional 16 Basic Cars in 1995; and an additional 3 Basic Cars in 1996, Citywide, to meet community needs" (Los Angeles Police Department 1997). Further assessments subdivided the original 18 policing Divisions into the current 21. "Community needs" thus comprise the statistical assessment of police territorial coverage and are coterminous with workload needs—if officers feel overworked in an area or mark the area as requiring special attention, this is what the community needs (Greene 2000). This data-driven territoriality was extended further during the tenure of William Bratton as Police Chief (2000–2009), who introduced the geographic crime-mapping program Compstat to which each area commander was responsible. In sum, we can meaningfully refer to the "18SLO029" community, map the streets, and pull up years of demographic and crime statistics, imputing through these measures community desires, needs, problems, and progress.

Two things are important to highlight. First, whatever else community might be, in an operational sense, it is grounded in the territorial imperative. That residents might constitute alternative conceptions of community—or advance alternative conceptions of space (see Herbert 1997)—is not relevant for police governance. Resident-centric notions of community are back-grounded or adjunctive to this schema. Second, while geography and community are not necessarily oppositional, this nexus has not been generated from, or in partnership with, residents. Rather it was revitalized from sociobiological theories and strategies of conflict and predation concerned explicitly with spatial control. The notion of community within community

policing is mobilized less to serve "the community," however that might be defined, and more toward a territoriality that arrogates geopolitical power to police. The ways that power can be used to determine the content of those spaces is taken up in the contemporary ethnographic analysis below.

PROBLEM SOLVING PARTNERSHIPS

Despite marking community-as-territory, in the political foment of 1992, administrators had to articulate how they would make police accountable to residents—a key component of community policing (Goldstein 1987; Skolnick and Bayley 1988). Proposals outlining strategies for community-police cogovernance and more general community-oriented rebuilding were rejected out of hand (Costa Vargas 2006; Davis 1993b).[3] The first step was to fix the Department's Chief to a renewable contract subject to approval by City Council. The second was community partnership, intended to keep police "accountable to all segments of the community" (Independent Commission on the Los Angeles Police Department 1991: 106). Obliquely referencing the uprisings, the LAPD immediately penned *Building Public Safety* (1992), describing the steps the department would take to "institute a 'new beginning' to build public safety confidence between the people of Los Angeles and their Police Department." The document asserts that the "community has a legitimate right to participate in the design, implementation, and assessment of public safety services," hinting at a robust and ongoing role for the community in reshaping the institution of policing.

Community-Police Advisory Boards (CPABs) are the only unit replicated within every Division specifically demarcated as a place for community-police strategic cogovernance. The main mechanism for realizing community partnership, CPABs are the direct descendants of the community meeting groups from the 1960s that characterized police efforts toward community under the original territorial imperative. Chief Bernard Parks pays homage to those groups in his

3 For example, see Costa Vargas (2006), which details the Coalition Against Police Abuse plan to independently elect a community review board with the power to subpoena and fire officers. This plan is still sometimes referenced at Police Commission meetings during the two minute "community comment" block.

Strategic Plan on Community Policing (1999), in which he declares that CPABs were established for ensuring a "continuing transmittal of information between the community and the police." CPABs "advise and inform the Los Angeles Police Department's Area Commanding Officers of quality-of-life problems and concerns in the community ... to share information and develop problem-solving strategies." This language, from a 2009 brochure entitled *Celebrating the Community-Police Partnership*, demonstrates the ongoing information provision element of CPABs overlaid with the cogovernance rhetoric from 1992: "The CPABs serve as advisory and problem-solving groups predicated on a community government philosophy" (Los Angeles Police Department 2009).

In reading community through CPABs, several roles for this unit are noted, none of which fit the description of "full partner" (Parks 1999) or "designer" of policy (Los Angeles Police Department 1992). First, police see community as a strategic resource while positioning itself as the problem solving actor at all geographic levels. The information that informs these solutions is partially, though not exclusively, from local participants. Soon after taking over command of the LAPD, Chief Williams made this clear: "The role of Community-Police Advisory Boards is to advise and inform Area commanding officers of community problems and concerns" (Williams 1993). Williams (1995) touts the "SARA" approach (Scanning, Analysis, Response, Assessment), which emphasizes a consideration of patterns, causes, consequences, and results in solving crime problems and sets officers as the locus of problem solving and data analysis (Center for Problem-Oriented Policing 2013). In contrast, the role of the community is that of complainant and data source.

Second, the informational relationship also comprises absorption and dissemination. CPAB members in 1992 were required to learn from the LAPD in a training program that continues (albeit unevenly) two decades later (Los Angeles Police Department 1992). The ethnographic data gathered for this study suggests that this is an opportunity to reorient community members into supporting police efforts, which they are expected to represent in their own neighborhoods (see Roussell and Gascon 2014). The community-police relationship can be summarized as follows: residents present police with complaints and information; the LAPD explains to residents how it polices and self regulates; residents represent these views locally. The core of this approach is largely unchanged from the 1960s and provides no mechanism of accountability for police nor any serious engagement with cogovernance, regardless of the community's "legitimate right to participate in the design, implementation and assessment of public safety services" (Los Angeles Police Department 1992). This contradiction between community political rhetoric and operational reality is perhaps best expressed by the public comments of Chief Parks regarding CPAB:

> Those community panels [CPABs], matched up with LAPD's geographic service divisions, "were never perceived to be a citywide political force that can out-vote captains, the chief of police, the commission," he said. Those advisory panels "are one of thousands of inputs" the Police Department uses in relating with citizens.
>
> (Pool 1999)

Despite the rhetoric of community empowerment marketed to LA residents after the violence of 1992, much of the community policing vision is a throwback to prior tactics and concepts developed in the 1960s. After a moment of crisis, the LAPD presented itself as a remade organization by highlighting the larger tropes of community policing within the threads of its past, notably the territorial imperative. Yet this vision for community policing had to pass public muster to maintain legitimacy after the uprisings and includes strong language on community cogovernance to preempt claims of a lack of accountability. To officers, community means territory; for residents, community is defined as CPABs. The word "community" is used liberally, but power is not returned to community residents. Instead, echoing Seattle, the concept is appropriated and residents are made responsible to the LAPD (Herbert 2005).

Anticommunity Policing: Race and Labor

Conceiving of community as territory enables a de-emphasis of the needs of residents in demarcated spaces, particularly when residents have little power to effect institutional change through partnership. The focus shifts from people to place. Those whose presence is coveted, useful, or simply tolerated can be discussed as "the community" against individuals and groups seen as problematic. Residents who come together with police to create community in CPAB meetings participate directly in this effort. This articulation of who is (and who should be) considered community is complicated by the presence of multiple meetings in South Division segregated by race and language. While the English meeting, composed mainly of black residents, is officially celebrated, the Spanish meeting of Latino residents is relegated to "outreach"; yet the Spanish meeting closely tracks the demographic changes occurring in South LA. This section uses the community/anticommunity framework to understand the logics of South Division's segregated meeting dynamic. It proceeds through three subsections, explaining first the themes that emerge from the English meeting and then those of the Spanish meeting. The final section details how LAPD uses its territorial prerogative to remake community by picking and choosing among these themes under its community mandate.

In "The Death of the Social," Rose (1996) argues that the "turn to community" is an emergent governance practice which legitimates the shift toward state disinvestment in the public welfare. He suggests that the state uses communities as repositories through which state power can be exercised while simultaneously absolved of its supportive responsibilities—the idea of community becomes a discursive tool to make palatable neoliberal social policy. Tactically, he indexes the rise of this community approach to the articulation of an "anticommunity," grounding claims to community against undesired populations. The appeal is intuitive: references to community conjure up notions of solidarity, togetherness, and nostalgia overlaid with a sense of consequence for the basic social fabric (e.g., Putnam 2000). In establishing CPAB, with a mandate to partner over neighborhood

concerns, police have provided a symbolic platform for residents to participate in constructing community in a way that encourages such bifurcations. It is against such anticommunities that community itself is constituted.

The official South Division CPAB meetings are usually attended by English-speaking CPAB members, other residents, neighborhood activists, business owners, and an ever-rotating cast of guests and speakers. Members are mostly older black residents, a very small contingency of middle-aged Latino residents with typically limited English abilities, and several local business owners (black, Korean, South Asian, and Latino). Division Captains and Senior Lead Officers take a direct hand in shaping the content of CPAB meetings. Agendas sometimes incorporate presentations from outside organizations, but more frequently highlight the work of special police units. Detectives from Vice discuss prostitution, juvenile kidnapping/smuggling, *casitas* (houses of prostitution and gambling), and abatement issues. One detective came to discuss domestic violence, but ended up explaining the realities of DNA evidence collection and processing compared to popular depictions. Gang Unit officers also sometimes present. These informative police presentations incorporate a certain level of marketing and attendees are directed to take their new knowledge back to their neighbors. Residents walk away with sharable information about the LAPD shaped by presentations from affable officials.

South Division's official CPAB meeting, conducted entirely in English, serves to give a voice to middle-aged and elderly black middle and working class residents. Many are local property owners who see a place for police in the ordering of their neighborhoods and simply want to engage in that process, regardless of their past or present activism. Some members are strongly loyal to LAPD and are unaware of challenges to police hegemony. This group lends police legitimacy within and outside of South LA, serves the two-way information transmission function by communicating messages from police to their neighbors, and provides a source for disorder complaints. These complaints are frequently lodged against illegal vending and day laboring, issues that impact the Latino community directly. Sometimes called "English CPAB," the meeting is loosely parliamentary with a resident co-chair and the Division Captain as permanent chair.[4]

The rising Latino majority in South Division also has a voice, but one that differs sharply from that of the English CPAB. The few Latino attendees at the English meeting are tokenized and largely excluded from collective discussions. Rather than hosting a single meeting invested with translation services or fashioning a systematic method of representation, police have opted to hold a separate Spanish-speaking meeting. Originally called "Spanish CPAB," in 2009 Captain Patton determined that there could be only one CPAB per Division, and the meeting became the ungainly "Spanish Speaking Community-Police Meeting," divesting it of official CPAB status. In 2010, under Captain Saitou, the meeting morphed into "Hispanic Outreach," where it has remained, going from a loose partnership meeting style to a more presentation-oriented style heavily regulated by police administrators. Hispanic Outreach is led by Hector Mendoza, an infrequent English meeting attendee, who exerts more direct control over the content and flow of his meeting than the resident co-chair does over CPAB. Moreover, in deference to the undocumented status of some of it attendees, the Spanish language meeting is largely anonymous, as opposed to the English meeting, which features background checks, membership badges, and fingerprinting for its members.

The two-meeting dynamic, coupled with the constant reshuffling of the Spanish meeting's status, provides insight into the interlocking issues of race, language, and citizenship underlying CPAB's community representation. Spanish-speaking Latinos are outsiders to CPAB in terms of language, but this outsider status carries over into the entire ethnic category as well. Latino residents not only lack leadership in the "official" CPAB meeting, but those who do attend are seldom consulted or speak up. Much

of this is a byproduct of the LAPD's strategic move to maximize Latino leadership talent in the name of outreach. Those Latino leaders responsibilized through this structure have all been used outside the formal structure of CPAB to increase turnout at Hispanic Outreach—which in turn lacks the status of the English CPAB meeting. As of 2013, no Latino resident had ever been appointed to any parliamentary position within the English meeting.

The roles of Latino and black residents within their respective meetings are defined differently. Black CPAB members are an important part of police image maintenance in the post-1992 era. In a world where gangs, violence, and crime are seen as primarily "black problems," the 1992 uprisings were seen largely as a black phenomenon, and black citizens remain outspoken critics of police brutality, it is symbolically important that the CPAB community of South LA remain primarily a body of black residents. Black CPAB members are agentive and legally aware individuals who can officially lay claim to a full set of citizenship rights. Although they share information and discuss with their neighbors, members seldom declare that they are speaking for the larger community, but rather that they are a part of a deliberative community body. They tend to arrive with the expectation of active participation in the CPAB process. As in any organization, there is a range of participation, but black residents stand ready to volunteer and make their presence known in an official capacity. They do not bring, for example, their children or other family members, since meeting time is devoted to official public business rather than the private realm of parenting. Having visible support from black residents remains crucial for maintaining police legitimacy after 1992; this, together with official markers such as background checks, contribute to elevating the community status of black CPAB members.

The increasing immigrant Latino majority in South Division, however, means that outreach is required in a way unnecessary for a population composed primarily of American citizens. The normative understanding of citizenship implies the ability to manipulate legal and civic process. Noncitizens have a harder time, and bringing Latinos "out from the shadows" (a commonly heard phrase), is a different process than placating

4 The resident co-chair and Division Captain positions changed twice and thrice respectively over the five-year observation period. Although co-chairs are nominally in charge, I have never witnessed a co-chair successfully introduce action contrary to police directive.

citizens demanding their rights. Latino residents attend Hispanic Outreach because of the direct benefits of learning about services, civic process, and immigration and to complain about crime and disorder, rather than because of any belief in the efficacy of the body itself. Hispanic Outreach encourages the broadest possible participation, including family members and holding a potluck supper afterward. Attendees at this meeting seem mainly uninterested in the business of cogovernance, no doubt because of the precarious relationship with citizenship that many experience. This is not to suggest that South Division's Latino population has no inclination to public service, but only that it may not be possible to express such an inclination within the police institution.

Consequently, Captains can shift the status of the Spanish language meeting without regard, because the population the meetings represent has no stake in the meeting as an institution. Although the idea of merging meetings is broached periodically, absorbing Latinos directly in the English meeting structure is functionally impossible, due to the different orientations, processes, and membership requirements. The function of Latino leaders like Mendoza is not to deliberate police engagement strategies, disseminate information to residents, or even to perpetuate the meeting itself, but to advise police on how best to encourage Latino governmental cooperation in ways that are accessible to immigrant families. In 2009, Mendoza had a private list of 300 names of prior meeting attendees, which comprised a strong portion of his value to police. Mendoza remains a power broker in a way that English co-chairs are not, but this status is just as precarious as the residents in whose name he advocates.

On the surface, the arrangements of CPAB and Hispanic Outreach suggest that black residents are feted by police for their image control potential, while Latino residents are largely marginalized. Yet the story is more complicated than this. The next section nuances the analysis by analyzing meeting content, engagement with community officers (SLOs), and the enforcement strategies discussed at CPAB. In hearing complaints of each group, police can pick and choose among the claims made in the name of community, retaining the ultimate authority in determining the demographic contents of their territory. These next sections demonstrate the fluid and relational nature of community and the ways in which the anticommunity is a product of racial perceptions and economic forces.

Regulating Latinos: Illegal Vendors and Day Labor

Hot button issues for the English meeting include vending, which is illegal in the City of Los Angeles, and the congregation of day laborers. Throughout English meetings, black residents use these issues to demarcate what they see as a growing Latino anticommunity. Although blacks and Latinos in South Division sell all kinds of things on the streets (e.g., counterfeit jerseys, bootlegged movies, clothes), discussions of illegal street vending refer almost exclusively to immigrant Latinos selling cooked and uncooked food items. Moreover, while there are some independent food carts, many vendors are franchisees of centralized organizations—vending is big, under-the-table business. Police expend little effort investigating the layers of capital investment involved in producing the thousands of food carts located around the city. Instead, the vendors themselves, the most visible exponents, bear the brunt of legal attention.

Street vendors' customers include many day laborers, and carts often orient around day laborer sites for customer convenience. Day laborers congregate in visible places, often near home improvement warehouses or parks, waiting for hourly employment. As well as attracting vendors, this creates nuisances and congestion for passersby, due to the large groups of Spanish-speaking men who engage in loud conversation, games, and gambling to pass the time between jobs. Food consumption and waste management become concerns. Many black residents see this as both a nuisance and a double standard, insofar as police do not hesitate to enforce anti-loitering ordinances at laundromats and other semi-public locations against black youth they presume to be unemployed. Day laborers are cited more commonly for their actual behavior rather than simply their presence.

The general feeling of the English CPAB is that illegal vending is a health hazard as well as a nuisance for traffic and noise. The disgust with vending is not just a feature of the practices themselves, but relates to the presence of Latino vendors in public space who serve as visible reminders of the changing face of the community. Vending becomes the entre for complaints about Latinos' labor market position more generally, as criticisms of vending's illegality are looped into the perceived legal and citizenship status of vendors. As Ms. Carter, a prominent CPAB member in her 80s, commented: "It really bothers me when they come down the street ringing that bell. This is illegal, they are felons just by being here." The issue is framed at the nexus of political economy and racial community politics:

After the meeting breaks up, I talk to co-chair Vera Fisher for a bit. She is still furious about the vending issue—or perhaps just venting about Latinos in general, it's hard to tell. Her main concern, she says, is that they don't pay taxes. Of course they pay sales taxes on their own purchases, which is a conversation she has apparently had with Linda and Hector Mendoza of Spanish CPAB, but there are taxes that legitimate businesses have to pay too.

Vera has a huge problem with remittances. She describes the local economy as a circle, with money circulating through consumers to local businesses to employees who become, or somehow pass on that money back to, consumers. Major corporations like Walgreens and El Pollo Loco centrally process their earnings and don't really put much money back into the community either, but Vera somehow manages to agree with that statement and make it support her argument as well. Remittances, in her eyes, are sucking money right out of the community and putting it into the places they [the vendors] came from.

(Roussell, fieldnotes, 2/11/10)

Vending comes to stand in for the labor market shift in South LA since the 1970s (Costa Vargas 2006; Sides 2003). Local small businesses, many of them black-owned, are seen to suffer as a result of the transitioning market and the degradation of black labor, while the proceeds of illegitimate businesses are funneled back to Mexico and Central America. Because vending is seen as ubiquitous (even police sometimes patronize mobile *taquerías*), Vera Fisher sees illegal vending as extracting money from the black community to support foreign economies, even as the labor market for black American citizens deteriorates. Cynthia Stacy, a former professor and vocal CPAB member, describes the difficulty in watching opportunities for black youth dwindle:

[The janitors] became unionized and then have been undermined by the Latino workers and there is tension there—it's economic. Now our kids—there are no Black kids working at McDonalds or even many younger kids, high school age kids working in the service industry, in the food industry, around our area because the adults [Latinos] who are more obtainable, are more employable. And they are working in fast food, so our kids have fewer opportunities for employment. ... I could go down the street [when I was younger] and there were my classmates working at the store, the drug store, the grocery store, whatever, it doesn't happen anymore.

The police response to vending complaints is enforcement, education, and accommodation. In keeping with the ethos of the territorial imperative, enforcement is a method favored by SLOs. Their enthusiasm is diminished only by the frustration over coordinating with the county Health Department in disposing of the carts. Ticketing is seen by vendors as "the cost of doing business," however, and many SLOs issue citations infrequently due to their lack of impact. The realities of time constraints, interagency organizing, and more pressing crime issues limit the frequency and scope of these sweeps. Perhaps recognizing these limitations, Captains and other LAPD administrators have begun to look toward education and accommodation. SLOs hand out flyers in Spanish to vendors before returning and those who speak Spanish sometimes warn vendors about upcoming sweeps. This makes some officers unhappy but is largely accepted with only minor grumbling.

Alongside the enforcement and grudging education by SLOs on specific issues are significant efforts to make Latino immigrants feel supported. In wrestling with the issues of vending and day labor, Captains have investigated different methods of compromise. One Captain publically supported creating a centralized farmer's market for vendors in South Division, while another Captain began efforts to collaborate in the building of a day laborer shelter with waste management facilities at a local home improvement retailer. More generally, police-sponsored presentations and events held through the U.S. Center for Immigration Services, the non-enforcement arm of federal immigration law, allow for information exchange and the beginnings of the citizenship application process for residents—another method of population regulation.

Police administrators argue this approach is necessary to engage immigrant Latinos in the criminal legal reporting process as witnesses and victims. LA is considered a "sanctuary city" due to Special Order 40 (enacted in 1979), which specifies that police ignore citizenship status in the performance of their duties, except in circumstances of serious felony law violation. During this fieldwork, police held or participated in several public discussions and explanations of immigration law and Special Order 40 (several in concert with the consulates of Mexico, Guatemala, El Salvador, and Honduras) to put noncitizen Latinos at ease in interacting with police. Despite this, many Latino residents continue to be skittish of police contact and their concerns are not groundless. Operations such as mid-day DUI checkpoints are suspected of camouflaging racist motives. Indeed, undocumented status is a tool that officers can use when convenient:

As the SLO reports wind down, Captain Patton mentions that he has gotten recent complaints from local businesses about illegal vending. The SLOs all attempt to address this simultaneously by speaking over one another, which is chaotic to record, but ultimately produces the following points: SLOs have made many arrests using bike cops, sweeping several areas, and turning all the names of "illegals" over to ICE [Immigration and Customs Enforcement]. Previously, only felons and gang members warranted a tip off to ICE, but they made an exception this time. Patton jumps in to justify this based on its effectiveness, although he says there was an uproar from members of the Latino community.

"Often though," Patton continues thoughtfully, "vendors are victims too, so maybe this is part of a broader issue."

(Roussell, fieldnotes, 4/9/2009)

Notably, although ICE was called in this case—illegally, under Special Order 40—the Latino community resisted this move and Captain Patton was induced to see vendors as victims, paving the way for the farmer's market and day labor facility initiatives that followed.

Indeed, after the violent beating of protestors at a May Day immigration rally in 2007, Latino participation at community policing events in South Division declined precipitously. Perhaps in part because of this loss of political potency in the Latino community, police administration—including South Division Captains, Chief Charlie Beck, and the LA Police Commission—has urged the reconciliation and accommodation that undergird South Division's efforts with Latinos. In sum, black CPAB members are partially successful in invoking their claims to community by denouncing the Latino-driven underground economy. Although these claims are grounded around the declining economy for black labor, this seems like a rearguard action in light of LA's structural adjustments. Enforcement, supported by the black CPAB community, is indeed used to regulate Latinos, but despite the lesser status of their community meeting, they are encouraged as the rising community. This enables Captain Patton to expand his definition of community to include vending Latinos as victims—and, thus, part of the larger Latino labor force.

Black Banishment: *Pandillas, Drogas,* and the *Lumpenproletariat*

If the attitude of police toward disorder crimes by Latinos can be characterized as grudgingly accommodating, the treatment of South Division's black population is not similarly ambiguous. Police use tips, information, and complaints from Latinos to connect gangs and drugs to South LA's black population, but in truth they do not need these things to continue such a campaign. Enforcement against gangs, drugs, and other offences continues apace—the problems that community policing was supposed to help ameliorate. Latinos stress blacks as a dangerous and disordered anticommunity, while reinforcing their own claims to community by defending vendors and day laborers as resourceful people who just want to work hard and earn an honest living. But the punishing of prostitution, homelessness, and those on parole and probation closely connects to the much larger tradition of punishing blacks in South LA.

Davis (1993a, 2006) describes various racist LAPD initiatives including Operation Hammer, where law enforcement mass-arrested black and Latino youth based on nothing more than their presence, and the LA Battering Ram, an armored tank used to break into the homes of suspected drug dealers. Costa Vargas (2006) describes the continuing indignities and beatings suffered by impoverished black men and women in South LA by police and other municipal authorities. The massive expansion in the scale of these control methods can be linked to the beginnings of LA's post-Fordism of the 1970s where black labor became seen as increasingly redundant and was shed in LA's structural readjustment (Sides 2003; Soja 2014). More recently, the subprime mortgage and foreclosure crisis of 2008 made a portion of LA's black population even more vulnerable by swelling the ranks of the homeless (Stuart 2011).

There are tens of thousands of gang members in Los Angeles, although estimates vary depending on definition and motivation.[5] In South Division, there are

black gangs, Latino gangs, and gangs without ethnoracial preference; some gangs are territorial, some sell drugs, and some participate in other types of crime, or fail to come to the attention of law enforcement at all. In Spanish, the word *pandilla* means simply "gang." Among the Hispanic Outreach attendees, however, *pandilla* stands in directly for black gangs and the gang violence and drug selling committed by black gangs. Supporting stereotypical narratives of black men as criminal, Latino attendees position themselves as crime victims and black *pandilleros* (gang members) that sell *drogas* (drugs) as the major source of fear in their communities.

Whereas black residents typically couch their concerns in discussions of language and legal status, Latinos tend to identify the objects of their complaints by race directly. *Afro-Americano* is used when speaking formally, but *moreno* and *negro* can be heard in side conversations, sometimes during Hispanic Outreach sessions, and in interviews. Latino residents describe both as impolite depending on the audience (i.e., acceptable around other Latinos, not around blacks). In general, Latino residents live and work alongside black residents (as well as the handful of white and Asian residents) and often maintain friendships and working relationships with them. Antipathy in meetings comes out most strongly in generalized references to gangs, gang members, and drug activity, nearly all of which are directed explicitly or implicitly at blacks as a group. Latino gangs are almost never the focus (even within the English CPAB). Below, Hector Mendoza guides Sgt. Sanchez, a temporary meeting host, and Tomás De La Garza in a stereotypical description of *pandilla* activity:

> Sgt. Sanchez throws out the statement that most crime is gang-related and that the rest is mainly domestic disputes of some kind or other. Gangs, he reminds us, operate through fear. They attempt to intimidate the community by writing on walls, getting tattoos on their necks, and forcing street vendors to pay "rent" or protection money. Somewhat contradictorily, he pushes us to "get involved" if we see a gang

---

5 CalGangs, the California system of recording gang affiliation, is not publicly available. Names are difficult to purge and the definitions of a gang member are somewhat loose. *The Guardian* puts the number of gang members in LA around 120,000 and this is general consistent with the LAPD's public presentations (Harris 2007).

member engaging in these behaviors. Gangs pick on those who are afraid, he says, those who don't call the police.

In the wake of this, Hector Mendoza reminds everyone of the taco venders on Culver and Jeffery St. who actually have little stickers given to them by the local gangs to advertise the fact that they pay rent. Angry at this protection scheme, Mendoza reminds us that "These people want to work!" Vendors have to fear the *pandilleros* as well as the police. Because the work is not strictly legal, vendors don't report the intimidation—so there is double fear for these people, he says, of both gangs and of arrest. If people come together and come forward, there would be more ability to move against gang intimidation. Tomás De La Garza takes the opportunity to speak as well, strongly and clearly informing us that gangs comprise *morenos*, and, as an afterthought, Latinos, who extort money from the community and sell drugs.

(Roussell, fieldnotes, 6/25/10)

South Division's transitioning demography ensures that local schools are strongly Latino—Vernon High School, where Abril Solis works, is more than 80 percent Latino. Although the school's constituency overlaps the territory of several gangs, both black and Latino, in discussing ethnoracial tension, Solis explains black *pandilleros* as directly responsible for school violence and the consequent dress code shift that enabled the identification and expulsion of black students:

Interviewer: The two get along well? The two groups? [Latinos and blacks]

Solis: There's been a lot of change, I don't know.

Interviewer: How was it before?

Solis: Well, we had a lot of fights because we had a lot of African American gangs.

Interviewer: And now that you have changed to uniforms, has this helped?

Solis: It's helped a lot because students can be identified ... before it looked like it might be a student but was not.

Interviewer: And they come in to do what? To sell drugs or start stuff?

Solis: Sometimes they came in grabbing and assaulting people, walking around with little bags [of drugs]...

While vending, for black residents, gathers together many cultural and labor market complaints against Latinos, Latino residents see the issue quite differently. For Latino residents, the illegal nature of vending is an issue only because it deters the reporting of other crimes. Vendors are understood as people attempting to earn a living through hard work rather than nuisances and threats to public safety. Vending easily slides into fear of labor market redundancy for black residents, while drugs and gangs stand in for Latinos' fear of blacks and crime, a fear that dovetails with the larger white polity. The outcome is a generalized fear of blacks, particular young black men, within neighborhoods that have only recently achieved majority Latino representation. Latino residents, although skittish of official engagement, decry black criminality as an anticommunity opposed to their own hardworking ethos.

Black Deterritorialization, Latino In-Migration

Both meetings operate around community/anticommunity demarcations, but as territorial enforcers police retain the ultimate prerogative in deploying the rhetoric of community. The meetings provide a space for the venting of complaints and the consolidation of community, but officers are under no obligation to adopt directly the perspectives of the attendees. Instead, they filter the complaints through institutional mandates and their own prejudices in regulating their territories. Observations suggest that, in the reverse of the accommodation of vending and day laboring, police support and even encourage Latino characterizations of blacks as a criminalized anticommunity. Working within the territorial imperative, officers deploy community rhetoric to deterritorialize what they see as black anticommunities.

Because concerns regarding *pandillas y drogas* are so ubiquitous and characterized as violent and dangerous, the ameliorating push for education and accommodation that tempers vending and day labor enforcement gains no traction. SLOs, the community policing officers-*cum*-mountain lions of the territorial imperative, play a strong role in organizing the deterritorialization of blacks within their territory. On ridealongs, SLOs spend most of their enforcement time targeting blacks, while openly lionizing the Latino work ethic. Black residents also comprise the general face of anti-police sentiment:

> After driving past [Section 8 housing unit], SLO Liz Fairbanks slows, stops, and points to what she calls a "rude house," full of Black folks who don't respect the police. They are not "police friendly." Worse, they teach their kids not to talk to police and that they are the enemy. "Hispanics," she says, aren't hostile like that. There are three people in plain sight as we roll by and they hold stock still and fix the car with a stare until we depart. Liz announces that she is offended by the fact that they don't wave to her.

> (Roussell, fieldnotes, 7/28/11)

Given a relatively free hand in determining the content of community within the borders of her BCA, Fairbanks uses the discretion granted to her under the auspices of community protection to play the role of "watchman" as specified under Wilson and Kelling's (1982) broken windows paradigm. The authors imagine their archetypical Officer Kelly like so:

> Sometimes what Kelly did could be described as "enforcing the law," but just as often it involved taking informal or extralegal steps to help

protect what the neighborhood had decided was the appropriate level of public order. Some of the things he did probably would not withstand a legal challenge.

> (Wilson and Kelling 1982: 2)

Like Officer Kelly, Fairbanks appropriates the mantle of community in challenging those she thinks do not belong by "ped stopping" them, all of whom, over the course of this same observation period, are black.

> SLO Fairbanks tells me several times that we can pull over and or "ped stop" anyone that I'd like. I'm fairly horrified by this and politely refuse several times. For example, we pass by a Black male youth casually riding a bicycle. She interprets his look—which I miss completely—as furtive, and seriously considers turning around and stopping him. I ask her why she would do this and she refers to her "spidey sense," saying that he looked "shifty-eyed." I gently push back without actually using the words "probable cause," but she baldly brings it up anyway. With a good knowledge of the rules of search and seizure and probable cause, she says, if she feels someone is suspicious, she can pull them over for any reason—biking on the wrong side of the road in this case—and having done that, she can then do whatever she wants.

> (Roussell, fieldnotes, 7/28/11)

Although Fairbanks gripes about vending throughout the day, over the course of that observation period, we "ped stop" three more people, all of them black and either homeless or appearing so, and have aggressive conversations with several more. This is not an unusual observation period. The constant refrain from SLOs in these instances is that they are simply enforcing community norms. Just before forcing an 18-year-old black woman out of his BCA for suspected prostitution, SLO Phil Hackett tells her this directly:

> SLO Hackett fixes her with a stare and says "Why am I unhappy?"

"Because I'm not paying taxes?" she offers.

"No," he says, "it's because you're on my street and the kids and parents around here don't want to see this."

He finally allows her to leave Jeffrey Avenue and head down a side street. In turning around, we pass her again, and he stops her again and quizzes her on where she's going—her uncle's house, which he ascertains is outside of his BCA. We speed away.

(Roussell, fieldnotes, 4/19/11)

Many white and Latino SLOs display clear anti-black attitudes or more subtle degradations toward black individuals seen as perpetrating disorder. Moreover, the dynamic is institutional: officers, for example, publicly answer simple questions like how best to capture the visual identity of a criminal suspect by illustrating through a generalized black subject.

Homeless individuals, prostitutes, and probationers/parolees especially are vulnerable to territorial policing. In revitalizing the Basic Car Plan and the territorial imperative, the LAPD built the NIMBY ("Not In My Back Yard") ethos right into its policing plan. On one level, this means that LAPD Divisions compete for crime decreases. On another level, individual SLOs acquire the incentive to chivvy their problems off onto other BCAs, particularly those in other Divisions. As Officer Hackett demonstrates, the presence of prostitutes can be addressed by physically relocating them outside of a BCA or Division boundary. Arrest is not uncommon, but the hassle of paperwork and processing time for a few nights in jail is often too much compared with the ease of ordering them one block over. Community improvement takes on the feel of a zero-sum game.

Further, while community members with jobs and property can be victims—indeed, this is officially constituted through typical CPAB complaints (Roussell and Gascón 2014)—the anticommunity is incommensurate with the idea of victimhood. Prostitutes were the targets of South LA's Grim Sleeper serial killer (active 1985–2007), but police made clear that, despite their residence and official victim status, they were not to be considered part of the community. The excerpt below depicts this dynamic in a freeform information session organized to collect resident knowledge for the Grim Sleeper investigation. Tensions run high, fear is palpable, and police hold the meeting because they are frustrated by a lack of investigative progress:

The next question comes from a black man in his mid-30s. His voice is a little high, as though he is a little frightened or perhaps a bit hostile. "There are a lot of people here—old, young—what message do you want us to take back to the community? Some people maybe are thinking about vigilante squads ... we've got to protect the sisters, because we're on edge. There's a lot of fear."

A cool answer comes from the officer in charge of the investigation. "No disrespect to the vics or their families, but the majority have been in compromising positions. Somebody knows something ... but no, no vigilante squads." I am taken aback by the callousness of this response. Some of the victims' family members are in the audience, have made themselves known, and are visibly distraught by the casual victim-blaming.

(Roussell, fieldnotes, 10/9/08)

The automatic response of the resident above is to fold the murder victims into a broad conception of the community, particularly given the presence of their family members. Yet the officer evinces disbelief that the community should be frightened, because the Sleeper only kills those found in "compromising positions." The community, in other words, cannot contain prostitutes.

Homeless individuals are also deterritorialized and discursively separated from the community, although as with vending these task forces must coordinate with the Health Department to dispose of possessions and encampments. Unlike vending, however, attempts at accommodation of the homeless by the English CPAB are met with stiff police resistance. Rather, Captain Patton induces CPAB to aid in deterritorialization by denying homeless people—or "cockroaches" in the parlance of one SLO—food and clothing in the hopes that they will migrate out of South Division, despite the co-chair's public observation that many are "from the neighborhood" and "just want to get it together." To foreclose community solidarity, Patton reminds the group of their class differences, emphasizing that "transients" enjoy their predicament and cannot thus be part of a partnership premised on normative community ideals. He refers to the police approach to homelessness, which comprises some sporadic attempts at service linkage together with conscripted labor, confinement, or banishment, as "tough love" (see also Beckett and Herbert 2009; Stuart 2011).

The LAPD's anti-black deterritorialization occurs not only under the purview of enforcement, but also as a direct function of their role as community expert and arbiter of territorial content. Incarceration is an obvious element of LA's black outmigration in the 1980s and 1990s (Costa Vargas 2006) and these trends continue; however, in the community policing era, police have the opportunity to play a larger role in composing community infrastructure. Within the territorial imperative, SLOs become experts to be consulted when larger governance issues impact their BCA. Officer Hackett outlines how his professional involvement in a municipal planning matter enabled him to operationalize a racial hierarchy of desirability:

SLO Phil Hackett laughs as we drive past where the new school is being built. "This," he says, pointing towards a dilapidated housing complex, "is where the 'I Hate Phil Hackett Club' lives." Due to his long tenure in his BCA, Hackett tells me that city planners consulted him on where they ought to put the new middle school. Since they were going to "eminent domain" the site and the housing therein regardless of location, they asked him which of three locations would have the best impact on crime. Hackett didn't hesitate to pick the multidwelling, low-income, predominantly Black housing complex. The city has since razed it, relocated many of the residents to the dilapidated complex that we drive past, and is building the school, as well as some new housing, where "many Mexicans have moved in," which he likes. The people he helped displace, however, aren't fond of him, he chuckles.

As if to illustrate his dislike of Black people by comparison, we immediately drive past another housing complex, which he informs me is home to a 23-year-old Latina immigrant of his acquaintance who owns her own hamburger stand and just opened another one. He uses this opportunity to compare Black people generally with the specific woman in the house—or, as he puts it, "200 years of oppression" vs. "one generation over the border."

(Roussell, fieldnotes, 4/19/2011)

Hackett's view, while blunt, is hardly rare. The discourse over Latino in-immigration constructs Latinos as victims of black crime, as deserving and hard workers (regardless of the legality of their work), and as necessary for the maintenance of LA's restructured economy. This leads to negotiations over how to "practice tolerance" toward the new arrivals—that is, how to regulate rather than banish. Latinos in South Division are seen as comprising a distinct group of laborers whose purpose is clear and necessary, if often unruly and sometimes necessitating sharp rebuke and selective deportation. Moreover, officers' racial biases regarding divergent Latino and black work ethics and crime propensities translate directly into accommodation or expulsion respectively.

Black residents, on the other hand, span the sharp division between the poles of community and anticommunity. CPAB members—mainly elderly, middle-class politically moderate activists—are feted for their political symbolism, consulted regarding disorder, and responsibilized to carry official messages to their neighborhoods. By articulating community standards within this governance framework, black CPAB members can induce certain forms of this anticommunity regulation against Latino disorder nuisances and confirm themselves as community. Police use this discourse to help shape a regulatory framework for Latino labor. Meanwhile, South LA's declining black population, disenfranchised in many arenas including employment and housing, constitute the main anticommunity. The unfolding logic of the territorial imperative allows the deterritorialization of black residents left behind by political economic restructuring and workplace discrimination.

Conclusion: Political Economy, Race, and Urban Governance

The past few decades have been characterized not only by the rise of mass incarceration, but also the expansion of its enabling processes—the increased surveillance, regulation, policing, and demarcation of urban space and impoverished black and brown populations. During that same period, urban governance has become dominated by themes of community partnership. Precisely because these trends seem antithetical, this article has attempted to explicate this relationship through the Los Angeles Police Department's community policing efforts in South LA. Policing is increasingly recognized as an important interlocutor within the framework of urban governance. Debates over how precisely to consider police within this matrix swirl between police as agents of the state and police action on the ground (Herbert 2006; Stuart 2011; Yarwood 2007). The purpose here is not to settle these debates, but rather to highlight the role of police in the urban demographic and social transformations required by the LA post-Fordist economy. Further, it is to situate the use of community rhetoric within such governance efforts as an important—and counterintuitive—means by which this occurs.

To make sense of the LAPD's community policing efforts, they must be emplaced within the broader economic and demographic trajectory of South LA. The past three decades of South LA's black-to-Latino demographic changes relate to LA's shift from a national manufacturing powerhouse to a bifurcated labor market. This move valorizes entertainment and technology industries on the one hand and on the other requires tractable undocumented immigrant labor. Black citizens, the last hired and first fired in LA's postwar boom, have seen unemployment rates reach 30–40 percent in the areas examined here (Marcelli, Pastor, and Jossart 1999; Sides 2003; Soja 2014; Soja, Morales, and Wolff 1983). Such economic alterations have historically produced state welfare rescue for poor white populations (Katznelson 2006), but here have produced deterritorialization and replacement. To think about the policing of race and labor market position is to see police as helping to process these economic shifts by encouraging and effectuating black-to-Latino demographic shift in South LA.

Community policing, the same initiative recommended to ease the racial tensions of LA's post-uprising era, is an important mechanism by which this occurs. Feelings of nostalgia and empowerment produced by the word "community" cover over a racial and economic project of control and exclusion extending from the larger neoliberal architecture of urban renewal, gentrification, and the staffing of a restructured economy. The violence of 1991–1992 may have laid the groundwork for such a governance shift, but the efforts of the state to restructure urban space have been the story of the past several decades irrespective of urban pacification (Lynch et al. 2013; Smith 1996). As numerous scholars have suggested, the drawing of community boundaries is a political act bound up in racial preference and concern for the needs of capital (Beckett and Herbert 2009; Davis 2006; Herbert and Brown 2006; Stuart 2014). Indeed, although Rose (1996) sees community as a vehicle for disinvestment, LA instead seems to be experiencing a shift in control mechanisms.

It is clear that we must consider urban economic utility and racial preference in discussing how threats to society are conceived and disposed of. As Brown (2010) has argued, the crucial question of who can be allowed to comprise "society"—or "community"—has animated these efforts toward reconfiguring urban space. The LAPD's decision to construct its community policing ethos around the socially Darwinistic territorial imperative seems entirely congruent with these dynamics. The operationalization of the territorial imperative in a partnership framework describes an informational process whereby residents in community meetings learn what police want and transmit that information back to them. In creating community partnership with residents, police retain the prerogative to regulate and expel in the name of community, picking and choosing among the complaints registered by black and Latino meeting attendees. Community is constituted in these meetings in a narrow sense, but is also relegated to these spaces when it comes to police deterritorialization of the anticommunity. Captains can thus consider reserving urban space for a literal market for Latino day labor while SLOs simultaneously authorize the razing of affordable housing units occupied predominantly by black residents—the result of which is to construct a public school attended mainly by the children of the Latino working poor. Community rhetoric, rather than a unifying force of resistance, identity, or creativity, contributes to demographic shift, not simply by accommodating Latino in-migration, but through black exclusion and removal. Community—reformulated through the territorial imperative—becomes a tool of governance corresponding to economies of race and labor desirability.

Although the role of community in state governance is an expanding subfield (Edwards and Hughes 2002; Herbert 2005; Rose 1996), it is important not to read these trends as entirely novel, but rather as a historical iteration of exploiting Latin American migrants and erasing black community self-determination (Ibarra and Carlos 2015; Muhammad 2010; Wilderson 2003). The focus on LA's economy here should not be taken as a challenge to more culturalist analyses of race, but rather as a supplement to them. The anti-blackness behind the civil death of the black subject, as Wilderson (2003) suggests, is "vital to civil society's political economy: s/he kick-starts capital at its genesis and rescues it from its over-accumulation crisis at its end" (238). Racial demographic shift has surely been a foundational part of LA's rescue from postindustrial crisis, accommodating Latino concerns, however grudgingly, at the expense of black residents. South LA's black residents, interpreted as unsuitable for a restructured service economy predicated on subpoverty wages and informal employment, are an anticommunity removed to make room for a vulnerable Latino proletariat. Deterritorialization

is consistent with anti-black racism, while Ibarra and Carlos (2015) remind us that the exploitation of Latino labor made desperate by U.S. trade and investment policy is an old story. Put another way, governmental rhetoric on community is made necessary by structural adjustment, but made possible by degrading urban black populations as the ultimate anticommunity.

The literature interrogating the logic of urban police govern-mentality is growing at precisely a moment when it is needed to provide insight on policing operations within poor neighborhoods of color. The strengths of the present analysis include its long-term duration, its naturalistic setting, and its location at the nexus of community discourse, racialized political economy, and law enforcement practice. Its limitations, including the localized scope and lack of black SLOs in the analysis, suggest directions for future research, as researchers address calls to diversify police forces and for national policing strategies (indeed, the isolation and scorn directed toward black SLOs only underlines some of these findings). While an impoverished section of Los Angeles is not universally generalizable, every geopolitical unit is vulnerable to the externalities of capital movement and its labor requirements, and these things are shaped by racial preference. Rising Latino labor power in cities beyond LA suggest that the social control mechanisms examined here may be worth considering in other urban locations as well. Empirical, on-the-ground examinations of the ways in which these structural shifts manifest themselves in different geographic settings can help frame and inform public debates on the uses, history, and present application of the law and its enforcement.

REFERENCES

Alexander, Michelle (2010) *The New Jim Crow: Mass Incarceration in the Age of Colorblindness.* New York: The New Press.

Alland, Alexander (2004) *Race in Mind: Race, IQ, and Other Racisms.* Hampshire, UK: Palgrave Macmillan.

Atkinson, Paul (2001) "Ethnography and the Representation of Reality," in Emerson, R. M., ed., *Contemporary Field Research,* 2nd ed. Long Grove, IL: Waveland Press, Inc. 89–101.

Beckett, Katherine, & Steve Herbert (2009) *Banished: The New Social Control in Urban America.* New York: Oxford Univ. Press.

Brown, Elizabeth (2010) "Race, Urban Governance, and Crime Control: Creating Model Cities," 44 *Law & Society Rev.* 769–804.

Center for Problem-Oriented Policing (2013) *The SARA Model.* Available at: http://www.popcenter.org/about/?p=sara (accessed 16 February 2013).

Costa Vargas, João Helion (2006) *Catching Hell in the City of Angels: Life and Meanings of Blackness in South Central Los Angeles.* Minneapolis, MN: Univ. of Minnesota Press.

Davis, Mike (1993a) "Uprising and repression in L.A.," in Gooding-Williams, R., ed., *Reading Rodney King/Reading Urban Uprising.* London, UK: Routledge, Inc. 142–56.

———(1993b) "Who Killed LA? A Political Autopsy," 199 *New Left Rev. I.* 29–54.

———(2006) *City of Quartz: Excavating the Future in Los Angeles,* 2nd ed. New York: Verso Publishing.

Edwards, Adam, & Gordan Hughes (2002) "Introduction: The Community Governance of Crime Control," in Edwards, A., & G. Hughes, eds., *Crime Control and Community: The New Politics of Public Safety.* Cullompton, UK: Willan Publishing. 1–19.

Emerson, Robert M. (2001) *Contemporary Field Research: Perspectives and Formulations.* Prospect Heights, IL: Waveland Press.

Emerson, Robert M., Rachel I. Fretz, & Linda L. Shaw (1995) *Writing Ethnographic Field-notes.* Chicago, IL: Univ. of Chicago Press.

Foucault, Michel (1995) *Discipline and Punish: The Birth of the Prison* (A. Sheridan, Trans.). New York: Vintage Books.

Gelman, Andrew, Jeffrey Fagan, & Alex Kiss (2007) "An Analysis of the New York City Police Department's 'Stop-and-Frisk' Policy in the Context of Claims of Racial Bias," 102 *J. of the American Statistical Association* 813–23.

Goldstein, Herman (1987) "Toward Community-Oriented Policing: Potential, Basic Requirements, and Threshold Questions," 33 *Crime & Delinquency* 6–30.

Greene, Jack R. (2000) "The Road to Community Policing in Los Angeles: A Case Study," in Alpert, G. P., & A. R. Piquero, eds., *Community Policing: Contemporary Readings,* 2nd ed. Prospect Heights, IL: Waveland Press, Inc. 123–58.

Harris, Paul (2007) Gang Mayhem Grips LA. The Guardian. Available at: http://www.guardian.co.uk/world/2007/mar/18/usa.paulharris (accessed 17 March 2007).

Herbert, Steve (1997) *Policing Space: Territoriality and the Los Angeles Police Department.* Minneapolis, MN: Univ. of Minnesota Press.

———(2005) "The Trapdoor of Community," 95 *Annals of the Association of American Geographers* 850–65.

———(2006) *Citizens, Cops, and Power: Recognizing the Limits of Community.* Chicago, IL: Univ. of Chicago Press.

Herbert, Steve, & Elizabeth Brown (2006) "Conceptions of Space and Crime in the Punitive Neoliberal City," 38 *Antipode* 755–77.

Hipp, John R., et al. (2010) *Ethnically Transforming Neighborhoods and Violent Crime Among and Between African-Americans and Latinos: A Study of South Los Angeles.* Los Angeles, CA: The John and Dora Haynes Foundation of Los Angeles.

Hughes, G., & Adam Edwards, eds. (2002) *Crime Control and Community: The New Politics of Public Safety.* Portland, OR: Willan Publishing.

Ibarra, Armando, & Alfredo Carlos (2015) "Mexican Mass Labor Migration in a Not-So Changing Political Economy," 15 *Ethnicities* 211–33.

Independent Commission on the Los Angeles Police Department (1991) *Report of the Independent Commission on the Los Angeles Police Department.* Los Angeles, CA: City of Los Angeles.

Johnson, Calvin C., & Jeffrey A. Roth (2003) *COPS Program and the Spread of Community Policing Practices, 1995–2000.* Washington, DC: The Urban Institute.

Katznelson, Ira (2006) *When Affirmative Action Was White: An Untold History of Racial Inequality in Twentieth-Century America.* New York: W. W. Norton & Company.

Lewontin, R. C., Steven Rose, & Leon J. Kamin (1984) *Not in Our Genes: Biology, Ideology, and Human Nature.* New York: Pantheon.

Los Angeles Police Department (1992) *Building Public Safety in Los Angeles.* Los Angeles, CA: City of Los Angeles.

———(1997) *LAPD Community Policing Implementation Plan.* Los Angeles, CA: City of Los Angeles.

———(1999) *Definition of Community Policing: A Staff Report.* Los Angeles, CA: City of Los Angeles.

———(2009) "Celebrating the Community Police Partnership," in Community Policing Unit, ed. Los Angeles: Los Angeles Police Department.

Loyd, Jenna M. (2012) "The Fire Next Time," 17 *City: Analysis of Urban Trends, Culture, Theory, Policy, Action* 431–38.

Lynch, Mona, et al. (2013) "Policing the 'Progressive' City: The Racialized Geography of Drug Law Enforcement," 17 *Theoretical Criminology* 335–57.

Marcelli, Enrico A., Manuel Pastor, & Pascale M. Jossart (1999) "Estimating the Effects of Informal Economic Activity: Evidence from Los Angeles County," 33 *J. of Economic Issues* 579–607.

Muhammad, Khalil G. (2010) *The Condemnation of Blackness: Race, Crime, and the Making of Modern Urban America*. Cambridge, MA: Harvard Univ. Press.

Myers, Randolph R., & Tim Goddard (2013) "Community-Driven Youth Justice and the Organizational Consequences of Coercive Governance," 53 *British J. of Criminology* 215–33.

Parks, Bernard C. (1999) *Strategic Plan on Community Policing: A Staff Report Prepared by Management Services Division, October 27, 1999*. Los Angeles, CA: Los Angeles Police Department.

Patillo, Mary (2003) "Extending the Boundaries and Definition of the Ghetto," 26 *Ethnic and Racial Studies* 1046–057.

Pool, Bob (1999) *Homeowners Chide Chief Over Cuts in Community Policing Plan*. Los Angeles Times. Available at: http://articles.latimes.com/1999/sep/18/local/me-11537 (accessed 18 September 1999).

Putnam, Robert D. (2000) *Bowling Alone: The Collapse and Revival of American Community*. New York: Simon & Schuster.

Richie, Beth E. (2012) *Arrested Justice: Black Women, Violence, and America's Prison Nation*. New York: New York Univ. Press.

Rose, Nikolas (1996) "The Death of the Social? Re-Figuring the Territory of Government," 25 *Economy and Society* 327–56.

Roussell, Aaron, & Luis D. Gascón (2014) "Defining 'Policeability': Cooperation, Control, and Resistance in South Los Angeles Community Police Meetings," 61 *Social Problems* 237–58.

Sides, Josh (2003) *L.A. City Limits: African American Los Angeles from the Great Depression to the Present*. Berkeley, CA: Univ. of California Press.

Skogan, Wesley G., & Susan M. Hartnett (1997) *Community Policing, Chicago Style*. New York: Oxford Univ. Press.

Skolnick, Jerome H., & David H. Bayley (1988) "Theme and Variation in Community Policing," 10 *Crime and Justice* 1–37.

Smith, Dorothy (2005) *Institutional Ethnography: A Sociology for People*. New York: AltaMira.

Smith, Neil (1996) *The New Urban Frontier: Gentrification and the Revanchist City*. New York: Routledge.

Soja, Edward W. (2014) *My Los Angeles: From Urban Restructuring to Regional Urbanization*. Berkeley and Los Angeles, CA: Univ. of California Press.

Soja, Edward W., Rebecca Morales, & Goetz Wolff (1983) "Urban Restructuring: An Analysis of Social and Spatial Change in Los Angeles," 59 *Economic Geography* 195–230.

Stuart, Forrest (2011) "Race, Space, and the Regulation of Surplus Labor: Policing African Americans in Los Angeles's Skid Row," 13 *Souls: A Critical J. of Black Politics, Culture, and Society* 197–212.

———— (2014) "From 'Rabble Management' to 'Recovery Management': Policing Homelessness in Marginal Urban Space," 15 *Urban Studies* 1909–925.

Valle, Victor M., & Rodolpho D. Torres (2000) *Latino metropolis*. Minneapolis, MN: Univ. of Minnesota Press.

Wilderson III, Frank B. (2003) "Gramsci's Black Marx: Whither the Slave in Civil Society?," 9 *Social Identities* 225–40.

Williams, Willie L. (1993) *Administrative Order No. 10: Partnerships for Community Policing*. Los Angeles, CA: Los Angeles Police Department.

———— 1995) *Community Policing*. Los Angeles, CA: City of Los Angeles.

Wilson, James Q., & George L. Kelling (1982) "Broken Windows: The Police and Neighborhood Safety," 249 *Atlantic Monthly* 29–38.

Yarwood, Richard (2007) "The Geographies of Policing," 31 *Progress in Human Geography* 447–65.

Zamudio, Margaret M., & Michael I. Lichter (2008) "Bad Attitudes and Good Soldiers: Soft Skills as a Code for Tractability in the Hiring of Immigrant Latina/os Over Native Blacks in the Hotel Industry," 55 *Social Problems* 573–89.

Racial Profiling of US Latinos by Local Police Officers

Lupe S. Salinas

This chapter focuses on the behavior of local and state police officers in the enforcement process insofar as alleged racial profiling is concerned. "Racial profiling" is the discriminatory practice law enforcement officials engage in when they target individuals for suspicion based on the individual's race, ethnicity, religion, or national origin. Criminal profiling generally involves reliance on a stereotype or a group of characteristics that police associate with criminal activity. For example, racial profiling utilizes the race of a person to determine which drivers to stop for minor traffic violations, practices commonly referred to as "driving while black or brown" (ACLU 2005). One of the earliest anti-Latino profiling enactments appeared in 1855 in a statute popularly known as the "Greaser Act" (Bender et al. 2008, 3). Whites commonly used the term "greaser" offensively to denote other disparaging labels like "mestizo" or "Mexican" (Pitt 1966, 309).

Anti-profiling policies traditionally prohibit focusing on a person as a suspect on the basis of her race, color, ethnicity, or national origin. An exemplary profiling law today bars law enforcement agencies from reliance on ethnicity, color, national origin, political affiliation, language, sexual orientation, gender, gender identity, disabilities, or medical conditions as reasons to stop or search people (Rodriguez 2009). When a police stop is based on suspect classifications such as race and ethnicity, the constitutional protections of the Fifth Amendment's due process clause (federal agents)[1] and the Fourteenth Amendment's equal protection clause (state agents)[2] are triggered.

In an *amicus curiae* brief presented to the Supreme Court, lawyers for the Mexican American Legal Defense and Educational Fund (MALDEF) described the Latino racial-profiling issue by stating, "It is not a crime to be of Mexican descent, nor is a person's Mexican appearance a proper basis for arousing an officer's suspicions. Those broad descriptions literally fit millions of law abiding American citizens and lawfully resident aliens" (Johnson 2010, 1019). MALDEF further asserted that a person's racial or ethnic background or appearance is a neutral factor in appraising probable cause or reasonable suspicion. Citing *Yick Wo v. Hopkins*,[3] the Latino civil-rights litigation firm rationalized that allowing police to base a decision to stop or search an automobile on the racial or ethnic appearance of the occupants would authorize the very same discriminatory law enforcement condemned by the Court (Johnson 2010, 1019). If Border Patrol agents can loosely decide who and what to search, experience establishes that they will naturally continue to focus on drivers of Mexican appearance, and on passengers who meet these ethnic criteria as the most likely targets for routine or random vehicle searches (Johnson 2010, 1019; Harris 2002, 4–6).

The Impact of Racial Profiling on America's Latino Population

Racial profiling of Latinos unfortunately continues today. It occurred well before Arizona's Senate Bill 1070 appeared in 2010. In fact, profiling of "Mexicans" dates back to the early years of the twentieth century, a fact documented extensively (Balderrama and Rodriguez 1995, 98–107; Salinas and Torres 1976, 873–75). Alleged lax enforcement by the federal government left state legislatures no choice but to implement immigration statutes to complement the federal effort. Once Arizona passed their statute, the copycats began. All similar state efforts have been vetoed by the federal courts on grounds that they interfere with the plenary power of Congress to regulate immigration.[4]

The Obama administration argued against state immigration-enforcement laws since they invite discrimination against many "foreign-born citizens and lawfully present aliens" (Mears 2011). The administration's position is admirable. In limiting their language to "foreign-born citizens," however, the Department of Justice overlooked the many native-born citizens who will continue to be victims of this degrading profiling. As the Arizona debate raged, American citizen Julio Mora was detained for hours without any facts to support suspicion.[5] In Texas, a county deputy stopped a vehicle in which Luis Alberto Delgado was a passenger. Delgado, a U.S. citizen who spoke only Spanish, showed his identification, but the deputy thought his birth certificate and social security card might be fraudulent and called in the Border Patrol (Carroll 2010).

Arizona also added a judge to the racial-profiling victims list. Jose Padilla, a Maricopa County Superior Court judge, was stopped twice. The officer never presented a citation or provided details as to the reason for the stop. At no time did the judge inform any officer of his official position. Judge Padilla concluded that his Latino appearance was the evident reason. The judge later complained to the police department involved. These incidents occurred even though the state had settled a lawsuit in 2006 against police officers where the proof indicated that vehicles driven by Latinos and blacks were significantly more likely to be stopped and searched than those driven by whites (Rubin 2008).

As previously mentioned, Julio Mora, an American citizen, along with Julian Mora, his father, a thirty-year resident alien, were detained on "suspicion" of undocumented status and fraudulent documents.[6] Julian Mora was driving to work when a county police vehicle forced an abrupt stop. The Moras were detained for three hours and released without charges (BBVM 2009). It is impossible for any officer to form a "reasonable suspicion" that the Moras were undocumented, or that they possessed fraudulent documents, merely by seeing them drive by a business where police were conducting an immigration raid. After all, according to the Supreme Court's guidance in *Terry v. Ohio*, police officers must be able to point to "specific and articulable facts" that, taken together with rational inferences from those facts, reasonably warrant a temporary stop and a limited frisk for weapons.[7]

Julio Mora testified before Congress about the discriminatory enforcement of the federal government's 287(g) program. Steve King, an Iowa Republican and a staunch anti-immigration politician, asked Mora "if the ordeal he experienced at the hands of the sheriff outweighed the tragic death of a young girl killed" by an undocumented drunk driver. Mora stood his ground, expressed sorrow for the father's loss, and told King that he wanted local police to enforce the law, but he only wanted for them to "be smart about it." In doing their work, he stated, police do not have to "detain American citizens and legal residents just because they happen to be Latino" (Lemons 2009).

In 2011, the federal district court granted the Moras' Fourth Amendment claim against the county for the unconstitutional stop and arrest.[8] Maricopa County later settled with the Moras (ACLU 2011; Lemons 2011). Altogether, in a period covering almost four years, litigants named Sheriff Joe Arpaio in 2,150 lawsuits in federal court and hundreds more in Maricopa County courts (BBVM 2009). The estimated bill to the taxpayers for Arpaio's policies through 2012 approximated $28 million (Ye Hee Lee 2012), an amount that will increase based on several alleged civil-rights claims pending, especially those arising in *Melendres v. Arpaio*,[9] in which the district judge found Arpaio to be liable. The county announced more settlements amounting to several million dollars at the end of 2013 (Ye Hee Lee and Kiefer 2013). Maricopa County voters, unfortunately, continue to reelect Arpaio and allow their tax money to contribute to his discrimination victims and their attorneys who assume litigation in these difficult cases.

Notwithstanding extensive comments about Arizona's less-than-fair policies, the state does not possess a monopoly on racial discrimination. For example, Nick Valencia, a CNN national news desk editor, encountered anti-Latino discriminatory treatment while attending a music festival in Atlanta, Georgia. When Valencia began speaking Spanish to some tourists from Mexico City, an Anglo woman told him to "go home," adding *vete* (leave) in Spanish, in case he did not understand English. Valencia stated that while he is an American first and a Mexican second, he lamented that he can never walk into a room and be "white," since to some people, the brown color of his skin means he is not even American (Valencia 2011).

The Chandler Roundup: State and Federal Cooperative Efforts in the Pre-287(g) Era

In Chandler, Arizona, instead of the *Terry*-type specific facts of criminal activity, a person's "Mexicanness" provided the justification for stops concerning immigration status by federal and state police (Romero and Serag 2005, 77). This enforcement effort, known as the Chandler Roundup, exemplifies the discrimination that Latinos experience as police agents seek shortcuts and engage in profiling in the detention and removal of unauthorized aliens. In 1997, prior to the formal initiation of federal-state cooperative agreements known as 287(g) programs, Chandler, Arizona, police collaborated with Tucson Border Patrol agents in detaining undocumented aliens. The operation led to multiple civil rights complaints that epitomize racial insults U.S. Latinos experience during immigration raids (Romero and Serag 2005, 77).

For example, a Latina left a supermarket, and the officer stopped her on the way to her car to ask for proof of citizenship. Police stopped another person while driving and asked for his papers. An agent asked another Latino to show proof of citizenship while he was pumping gas. In contrast, the agent did not question the Anglo couple pumping gas nearby. Additional proof surfaced that "Mexican appearance" became the "criminal behavior" that justified the stops. Agents had inserted the words "Mexico" and/or "Mexican" in the "deportable alien" form before the dragnet even began (Romero and Serag 2005, 82, 84 n. 52).

In response to complaints, the Arizona state attorney general conducted an investigation. The Chandler Roundup report analyzed complaints made by 71 Latinos. Out of those 71 complainants, 41 were detained on alleged unauthorized presence. According to the recorded status of the 41 detainees, 11 were U.S. citizens of Mexican ancestry, 16 were authorized Latino residents, 3 had work permits, and 11 were undocumented (Romero and Serag 2005, 84). In other words, 73 percent of the stops involved persons entitled to be in the United States.

An additional example of extreme racial discrimination involved Chandler police who went to a trailer home without a search warrant. The police told the residents that the park manager had given them a map and marked where the Latinos lived. An occupant asked police if they had a right to enter, and they basically justified their warrantless entry on the grounds that people living there were allegedly "here illegally." As it turned out, all the occupants had a right to be in the United States (Romero and Serag 2005, 87–88).

Police and politicians frequently assume that undocumented persons lack constitutional rights. They are incorrect. The Fourth Amendment and judicial opinions provide protection from unreasonable searches and seizures for all persons, including undocumented aliens.[10] The Chandler police chief defended his tactics during the five-day raid by asserting that the procedures were "no different than everyday experiences of all U.S. citizens crossing the border" (Romero and Serag 2005, 85). The chief, as the head of a police department, disregarded a critical distinction he should know: stopping and questioning a person—any person—about their citizenship is justified at the border since the border entry poses a much greater security risk to our country than detaining a person in Chandler, 120 miles from the border (Romero and Serag 2005, 86–88). The city eventually settled a lawsuit arising from this illegal activity (Vargas 2002, 796).

The 287(g) Program and the Exacerbation of Latino Racial Profiling

In the 1996 immigration statutes, Congress provided local governments with immigration enforcement powers by providing for collaborative 287(g) agreements, also referred to as memoranda of understanding.[11] Previous Department of Justice (DOJ) policy statements declared that state and local police lack authority to stop and detain an alien solely on suspicion of "civil deportability" (U.S. Department of Justice 1996), a perspective that changed after 9/11 when the federal government needed the assistance of local police to combat terrorism. In the process, however, 287(g) programs inadvertently allowed the injection of local anti-immigrant prejudice into immigration enforcement. Participation by some clearly racist county sheriffs exacerbated the already existing anti-immigrant hysteria (Stelter and Carter 2009), a mix that inevitably resulted in racial profiling and other civil rights abuses.

Section 287(g) formalizes the ability of the states and the federal government to enter into Memoranda of Understanding[12] in the performance of immigration-officer functions.[13] A subsection clarifies that a federal-state agreement is not required for a state employee to communicate with the attorney general regarding the immigration status of any individual, or to cooperate with the federal authorities in the identification, apprehension, detention, or removal of aliens not lawfully present in the United States.[14]

The 287(g) agreements have led to many complaints from civil rights groups and Latino victims. An immigrant-rights activist claimed that the program has been tainted by rampant mismanagement and racial profiling on the part of various lawmen, particularly Joe Arpaio, who ran the nation's largest program (Weissman, Headen, and Parker 2009). Others complained that the secretary of Homeland Security had expanded the program notwithstanding the evidence of abuses by local police. Designed as an effort to remove "illegal criminal aliens" from the United States, the 287(g) programs instead have become synonymous with human rights abuses. The executive director of the National Immigration Forum stated that the program essentially allowed "local cowboys to round people up in immigrant communities" (Ruiz 2009).

A significant number of the nation's large-city chiefs of police oppose 287(g) programs. These officials have called on Congress to fix the broken immigration system, and condemned the use of local police as immigration agents. Their primary apprehension centers on losing the confidence and cooperation of immigrants in coming forward as witnesses with regard to regular street crime, such as homicides. The chiefs have given community safety a higher priority (Ruiz 2009).

In 2009, North Carolina law professor Deborah Weissman provided a statement regarding state and local enforcement of immigration laws in North Carolina before the House Judiciary Committee's Subcommittee on the Constitution, Civil Rights, and Civil Liberties (Weissman 2009). In her report, she discussed the detrimental impact of 287(g) programs, which includes the tolerance of racial profiling and stereotyping; an apprehension about dealing with law enforcement, thereby compromising public safety for all (Pham 2004, 983); the economic damage to already financially strapped municipalities as immigrants flee these communities and create a loss of profits for businesses and a decrease in tax revenues (Pruitt 2009, 152–53); and the violations of basic American liberties that have a tendency to include resident aliens and citizens alike in the deportation process (Weissman 2009). Notwithstanding the stated goals of the 287(g) programs, i.e., to target dangerous criminals, the data reveal that the majority of undocumented immigrants snared in North Carolina's 287(g) project committed traffic infractions and low-level misdemeanors (Weissman 2009).

In Alamance County, North Carolina, approximately 70 percent of the detained immigrants were held for routine traffic offenses. The numbers should not shock anyone considering that local law enforcement set up roadblocks to check licenses near Latino markets on the weekends and stationed themselves on Sundays at roads that provide access to Latino churches. Under these circumstances, the slight odds of finding anyone engaged in criminal behavior instead reveal a decision to profile Latinos racially for minor matters (Weissman 2009).

These questionable law-enforcement activities prompted the DOJ's Civil Rights Division to request Alamance County Sheriff Terry Johnson to amend the county's policing practices to diminish the possibilities of violating constitutional rights of Latinos (Perez 2012). The DOJ gave the sheriff time to respond as to what the county would do to avoid Fourth Amendment unreasonable seizures. The sheriff's attorney then responded with a general denial (Kitchen 2012), and the DOJ filed a lawsuit against the sheriff and the county (U.S. Department of Justice 2012b).[15]

The DOJ advised Sheriff Johnson and the Alamance County Sheriff's Office (ACSO) in North Carolina that federal investigators found reasonable cause to believe that ACSO engaged in a pattern or practice of discriminatory policing against Latinos. These activities included targeting of Latino drivers for traffic stops, a claim based on a study that deputies were between four and ten times more likely to stop Latino drivers than non-Latino drivers. In addition, deputies routinely located checkpoints just outside Latino neighborhoods, forcing residents to endure police checks when entering or leaving their communities. In the event non-Latino drivers entered the checkpoint, deputies would allow these drivers to pass through without showing identification while deputies examined identification of all or most Latino drivers (Perez 2012, 3, 4).

The Alamance County study also indicated that deputies arrest Latinos for minor traffic violations, but they issue citations or warnings to non-Latinos for the same violations. The DOJ revealed evidence that Sheriff Johnson directed his supervisory staff to inform subordinates, "If you stop a Mexican, don't write a citation, arrest him" (Perez 2012, 5). The DOJ investigation revealed that the sheriff and his leadership explicitly instructed deputies to target Latinos with discriminatory traffic stops and other enforcement activities (Perez 2012, 5; Fox News Latino 2013). This contributed to jail booking and detention practices that conveniently led to discriminatory immigration-status checks of Latinos. Eventually, the department accused the sheriff and his supervisors of fostering a culture of bias by using anti-Latino epithets, such as calling Latinos "taco eaters" and describing them as morally depraved drunks (Perez 2012, 6).

The Weissman Report also addressed the discriminatory administration of a facially neutral program. Professor Weissman referred to North Carolina's "traditions of white supremacy," which, in combination with the 287(g) memorandum of understanding, often contributed to anti-Latino hostility and racial bigotry. The Alamance County Commissioners Court, for example, enacted a resolution calling for a moratorium on further immigration to the county. In addition, Johnston County Sheriff Steve Bizzell complained that immigrants breed "like rabbits," and ACSO's Terry Johnson called "Mexicans" sexual perverts. Not surprisingly, during May 2008, one county's ICE-authorized officers charged 83 percent of the immigrants arrested with traffic violations, raising concerns about serious civil rights and liberties issues (Weissman 2009).

In another part of the nation, an Irving, Texas, study of the effects of the Criminal Alien Program (CAP) revealed that racial profiling of Latinos increased once the city became a working partner with U.S. Immigration and Customs Enforcement (ICE) in 2006. Congress made it clear that the collaboration program should be geared to removal of aliens with "serious criminal histories." Once CAP began its operation, a study of the detainees held by Irving police revealed that only 2 percent of the charges were for felony offenses, while 98 percent involved misdemeanor offenses. Another disturbing statistic revealed that arrests for misdemeanor cases were significantly more for Latinos than for whites or African Americans. Finally, the records disclosed that between April and September 2007, the number of Latinos stopped by Irving police for petty offenses (punishable by fine only) increased by almost 150 percent, indicating that racial profiling played a major role in the stops and the enforcement. Once community groups protested, the seizures decreased (Gardner and Kohli 2009, 2, 5–6).

Based on extensive complaints of civil liberties violations, ICE reviewed the 287(g) programs.

Notwithstanding these allegations, Secretary of Homeland Security Napolitano announced in October 2009 collaboration with sixty-seven state and local law-enforcement agencies. These agencies pledged to improve public safety by joining ICE to provide a larger immigration enforcement effort, and by concentrating on the detention of criminal aliens who threatened local communities (U.S. Department of Homeland Security 2009).

The removal numbers reflect that the five top nations of origin are all Latin American, accounting for almost all the removals and indicating some possible profiling in order to reach these percentages. Based on their numbers, Latinos account for at least 95 percent of all persons removed during the 2012 fiscal year. Of the total 419,000 persons removed, the top sending nations totaled 400,000 persons. The number one nation, Mexico, accounted for 73 percent of all Latinos removed.

At the same time, only 50 percent of those Mexicans had criminal-related bases for removal, compared to 45 percent of all deportees for that year.

Constitutional Foundation for Racial Profiling

America's racial and ethnic profiling problems emanate not only from the prejudice of human beings but also from our nation's Supreme Court rulings. In *Terry v. Ohio*, the Court created the reasonable-suspicion exception to the probable-cause standard of the Fourth Amendment.[16] If an officer has knowledge of specific and articulable facts that leads to a reasonable suspicion of criminal behavior, the agent may conduct a temporary detention, even of a vehicle.[17] If the person reasonably appears to be a threat and possibly armed, the officer can conduct a frisk of the individual for officer protection. The officer assesses the reasonable inferences and utilizes his or her experience in determining if there is a reasonable, articulable basis for acting. However, this suspicion cannot be based upon an "inchoate and unparticularized suspicion or 'hunch.'"[18]

In *Whren v. United States*, the Court responded to allegations of a possible pretextual traffic stop by

District of Columbia officers in a neighborhood noted for its high drug activity.[19] The officers in an unmarked car became suspicious after witnessing a truck waiting at a stop sign for more than 20 seconds.[20] During this stop, the truck's youthful driver looked downward towards the passenger's lap. The police turned and headed back towards the suspicious vehicle. The truck then turned without signaling and sped off at an "unreasonable speed," and police caught up to the vehicle at a stoplight.[21] As the officer stepped up to the truck window, he observed two large bags of what he believed to be crack cocaine in Whren's hands.[22]

Whren alleged that the stop was not justified by probable cause, and that the officers' reasons for approaching the vehicle were pretextual.[23] Whren conceded that the officer had probable cause for traffic violations.[24] Whren and his partner in crime, both of African American descent, asserted that a traffic violation should not suffice, since officers will succumb to utilizing traffic stops to discover other law violations in the absence of probable cause or even reasonable suspicion, and resort to an impermissible factor such as the occupant's race.[25] The Supreme Court ruled that an officer can stop a vehicle if a traffic violation has been committed, and evidence discovered would be admissible, even if the officer made the stop to discover possible criminal activity.[26]

Terry and *Whren* are generally regarded as two cases that largely facilitated racial profiling. Obviously, minority profiling has occurred since time immemorial. To aggravate matters, particularly for Latinos, the Supreme Court decided an immigration detention case shortly after *Terry*. In *United States v. Brignoni-Ponce*, federal officers stopped a vehicle based on the Mexican appearance of the driver and occupants. The Court addressed the permissibility of an officer on a roving patrol making such a stop when the only articulable fact was the occupants' Mexican ancestry (Romero 2000).[27]

The Court rejected this exclusive police reliance on the ethnicity of the persons in the vehicle. The Court specified that at locations away from the border and its functional equivalents, roving patrol officers may stop vehicles only "if they are aware of specific articulable facts, together with rational inferences from those facts, that reasonably warrant suspicion that the vehicles contain aliens who may be illegally in the country."[28] The Supreme Court in *Brignoni-Ponce* deemed the stop and interrogation not "reasonable" under the Fourth Amendment.[29]

The Court added that approval of "roving-patrol stops of all vehicles in the border area, without any suspicion that a particular vehicle is carrying illegal immigrants, would subject the residents of these and other areas to potentially unlimited interference with their use of the highways, solely at the discretion of Border Patrol officers."[30] The Court cautioned that significant numbers of native-born and naturalized citizens have the physical characteristics identified with Mexican ancestry.

The Court's prohibition of an exclusive ethnicity basis for stopping a vehicle sounded like an excellent approach for the protection of a Latino's civil rights. However, the majority opinion opened the legendary Pandora's box when it conceded that "Mexican appearance" constitutes a relevant factor when considered

with other specific and articulable facts. With that language, the Court granted flexibility to those officers who were inclined to focus on persons of Latino descent. As Judge Posner wrote thirty years after *Brignoni-Ponce*, "Whether you stand still or move, drive above, below, or at the speed limit, you will be described by the police as acting suspiciously should they wish to stop or arrest you. Such subjective, promiscuous appeals to an ineffable intuition should not be credited."[31] In this fashion, the intended *Brignoni-Ponce* protections dissipated, and Latinos continued being subjected to stops and questions about their immigrant status.[32]

Terry introduced the reasonable-suspicion concept that allowed a police officer to detain a person briefly.[33] *Brignoni-Ponce* extended this standard to the immigration enforcement agent.[34] Today, with the advent of federal-state cooperative agreements under Section 287(g), the same standard is available for thousands of police officers across the nation in collaborative efforts with federal agents.[35] *Brignoni-Ponce* allows ethnic appearance as well as other factors that could collectively lead agents to find reasonable suspicion based upon "specific articulable facts" (Gowie 2001, 233).

For instance, agents can consider the characteristics of the area where they encounter a vehicle, its proximity to the border, and their knowledge of alien traffic in the area.[36] Law enforcement can also take into account any of the following: (1) the behavior of the driver (e.g., erratic driving or attempts to evade officers); (2) the type of vehicle and its transportation use (e.g., station wagons with large compartments for fold-down seats or spare tires); or (3) a vehicle's outward appearance (e.g., one heavily loaded or carrying an "extraordinary" number of passengers).[37]

In a somewhat exaggerated comment about the twists and turns on the road to racial profiling, the *Brignoni-Ponce* Court concluded by stating: "The Government also points out that trained officers can recognize the characteristic appearance of persons who live in Mexico, relying on such factors as the mode of dress and haircut."[38] The Court never explicitly approved this claim, but the mere mention of this dictum, or illustrative comment, has been unfortunately used and abused since this decision.

These words about a certain "mode of dress and hair-cut" were entirely unnecessary for the decision of the case. Not surprisingly, years later Arpaio justified his unlawful actions when he pledged to continue removal of persons whose "clothing, accents and behavior betrayed them as likely illegal immigrants" (*New York Times* 2009).

A Critical Assessment of the *Terry v. Ohio* Reasonable Suspicion Abuse

"Not all Latinos are undocumented persons, and not all undocumented persons are Latinos" (Salinas and Colon-Navarro 2011, 5). Since Latinos constitute the largest ethnic minority in the United States, this premise is especially significant. Ethnic appearance is *not* evidence of criminality. In fact, ethnicity should not be a factor, with the exception of those *criminal* investigations in which the suspect's ethnicity constitutes part of the probable-cause information. Our nation fought Nazi Germany in great part because of the dictatorial profiling, harassment, and efforts to annihilate the Jewish people. Those horrific experiences should teach any freedom-loving people that policies that authorize police to detain a person to see his "papers" can only be seen as an "unreasonable" practice that violates general rights to privacy and freedom.

After almost forty years since *Brignoni-Ponce*, complaints of police detentions based on ethnicity or on lack of reasonable suspicion of criminal activity continue (Carroll 2010). The violations of constitutional rights adversely impact not only undocumented persons but also lawful resident aliens and native-born United States citizens. All "persons" that make up these three U.S. Latino population groups are entitled to protection against unreasonable searches and seizures.

In *United States v. Zapata-Ibarra*, Fifth Circuit Judge Jacques Wiener passionately expressed his objections to judicial violations of these rights in a case from the border area with Mexico. The jurist, in a case involving the "reasonable suspicion" concept, wrote a dissenting opinion against the claim that probable cause existed.[39] The judge quite passionately conveyed how perturbed he was by the haphazard method by which federal courts were upholding allegations of reasonable suspicion and essentially converting them into probable-cause findings.[40]

Judge Wiener expressed grief that the court had supplemented the Fourth Amendment's proscription of unreasonable searches and seizures with a caveat, "except in proximity to our border with Mexico."[41] He complained how the government's "so-called War on Drugs and its efforts to interdict illegal immigration" had led to a "public hysteria that has in turn impeded rational judgment and logic."[42] Judge Wiener criticized the "evisceration" of Fourth Amendment protections along the Mexican border, and classified immigration-stop cases as being in the same category as the racially based internment of Japanese in concentration camps during World War II.[43] He referred to this case as an example of the judiciary's shameful failure to defend constitutional civil liberties "against the popular hue and cry that would have us abridge them."[44]

Judge Wiener then expressed how the federal courts had encouraged officers to "engage in the charade of 'articulating facts' just so that we can point to something as the underpinnings of our retrospective findings of 'reasonable suspicion' when judges uphold vehicle stops that otherwise offend the Fourth Amendment."[45] The jurist proceeded to describe how prior decisions inconsistently justified stops: "The vehicle was suspiciously dirty and muddy, *or* the vehicle was suspiciously squeaky-clean; the driver was suspiciously dirty, shabbily dressed and unkempt, *or* the driver was too clean; the vehicle was suspiciously traveling fast, *or* was traveling suspiciously slow." Judge Wiener adds that the opinions additionally assert that the vehicle—of whatever type—is the kind of vehicle typically used for smuggling aliens or drugs. Furthermore, other reasons for the stop included "the driver would not make eye contact with the agent, *or* the driver made eye contact too readily; the driver appeared nervous (*or the driver appeared too cool, calm, and collected*)." Also, "the vehicle was riding suspiciously low (overloaded), *or* suspiciously high (equipped with heavy duty shocks and springs); the passengers were slumped suspiciously in their seats, presumably to avoid detection, *or the* passengers were sitting suspiciously ramrod-erect," and on and on, ad nauseam.[46]

Judge Wiener then explained how, in a prosecutorial effort to justify the temporary detention and then permanent seizure based on the facts in the instant case, the agent provided statistics that established approximately 200 detentions, which resulted in 30 apprehensions on the rural road at issue.[47] The judge exclaimed: "Bragging about netting 30 apprehensions out of 200 stops is analogous to a major league baseball player's bragging about a .150 batting average—hardly an all-star performance."[48] In other words, the judge noted that the officer made erroneous stops in 85 percent of the contacts with "suspects."[49] He then clarified that he was not criticizing his colleagues of the panel majority, or the agent who stopped Zapata-Ibarra: "Rather, the bone I pick is with the judiciary as a whole for the part we have played and continue to play in rolling back the Fourth Amendment."[50] More than a decade has passed since Judge Wiener expressed his frustrations. Sadly, innocent U.S. Latinos are still being subjected to violations of their Fourth Amendment rights.

"Mexican" Appearance as a Permissible Factor: A Judicial Remedy for the Twenty-First Century

The principle enunciated in *Brignoni-Ponce*—that Mexican appearance is permissible in determining reasonable suspicion—must be judicially and legislatively discarded. In 1975, *Brignoni-Ponce* sacrificed Latinos and permitted their ethnicity to serve as an articulable fact in the reasonable-suspicion formula. In 2000, the Ninth Circuit appellate court considered the geometric Latino population growth over three decades and decided to eliminate ethnicity from the *Brignoni-Ponce* reasonable-suspicion standard.

One remedial step will require the Supreme Court and the lower federal courts to interpret the Fourth Amendment by providing a practical meaning to the word "reasonable." The decision in *Terry*, as written, can possibly be applied fairly, but judges must be steadfast in their adherence to the Fourth Amendment. The police action must be taken on the basis of *specific and articulable facts*, and not on conjecture as to the status of a person. Judge Wiener's scathing dissent condemns creative police and indifferent jurists who have misapplied *Terry*.

Brignoni-Ponce explicitly allowed Latino ancestry, coupled with other factors, to justify reasonable suspicion if agents overall found specific and articulable facts that suggested a belief that a crime was either in the planning process, in progress, or completed. As time passed, judges became lax and began to permit too much leeway in what constituted reasonable suspicion. Once the words "specific and articulable facts" began to be disregarded, the violations described by Judge Wiener proliferated.

Brignoni-Ponce Reconsidered: The Latino Population Increase and Violations of Rights

In the year 2000, California's Ninth Circuit appellate court provided a remedy to offset the increased Latino racial profiling. In *United States v. Montero-Camargo*, the *en banc* Court of Appeals concluded that *Brignoni-Ponce's* principle had become obsolete as to California-based cases. The court considered the

U.S. Latino population growth as compared to the *Brignoni-Ponce* 1970 Census figures. The Ninth Circuit decided that this population increase diminished the probative value of Latino ethnic appearance, especially where particularized or individualized suspicion is required.[51] The full court further cautioned that "in an area in which a large number of people share a specific characteristic, that characteristic casts too wide a net to play any part in a particularized reasonable suspicion determination."[52]

The Supreme Court denied the petition for review, known as certiorari, effectively departing from the *Brignoni-Ponce* standard.[53] Under Court practice, however, this refusal to hear the appeal has no precedential effect. In other words, the denial of certiorari does not establish a national standard regarding the use of ethnicity as an articulable fact. Instead, the ruling is applicable only to the states in the Ninth Circuit's jurisdiction.[54]

In *Montero-Camargo*, the district court found a sufficient basis for the investigatory vehicle stop and denied the motion to suppress the marijuana.[55] The regular panel affirmed. Both courts allowed the Latino appearance of the occupants as a factor to prove reasonable suspicion.[56] The Ninth Circuit panel *en banc* reviewed the regular panel's ruling and affirmed that police had reasonable suspicion to stop the vehicles to investigate further.[57] The full panel, however, reversed the part of the opinion that ratified Latino ethnic appearance as a valid specific and articulable fact.

After eliminating the Latino ethnic factor, the *en banc* court ruled that the totality of the other facts nevertheless sufficed to establish reasonable suspicion.[58] By concluding that ethnicity was relevant, the district court and the regular panel relied on outdated demographic information.[59] The *Brignoni-Ponce* Court referred to the almost 4 million Latinos in 1970 in the states bordering Mexico.[60] *Montero-Camargo* reasoned that the 2000 Census data of 34 million Latinos nullified the *Brignoni-Ponce* dictum.[61] In the following decade, when profiling concerns became more acute, the 2010 Census population counted 50.5 million Latinos (Passel, Cohn, and Lopez 2011).

In conclusion, the *Montero-Camargo* ruling is even more critical for the protection of Latino rights. In that regard, the Supreme Court should make *Montero-Camargo* the national rule. In the alternative, Congress should legislate that the *Montero-Camargo* standard bars the general resort to race or ethnic origin as a basis for reasonable suspicion or probable cause.

Maricopa County's Racial Profiling Declared Invalid in *Melendres v. Arpaio*

The Supreme Court voided three provisions of Arizona's S.B. 1070 in *Arizona v. United States*[62] since these sections conflicted with the federal government's plenary immigration-enforcement power. The voided sections required all immigrants to obtain or carry immigration registration papers, made it a state criminal offense for an unauthorized immigrant to seek work or hold a job, and allowed police to arrest suspected undocumented immigrants without warrants.[63] The Court nevertheless allowed a controversial provision that requires police to check the immigration status of someone they suspect is not present with federal permission.[64] The justices refused to enjoin this section since it had not gone into effect and state courts had not had an opportunity to construe it.[65]

A federal court later ruled in Maricopa County (Phoenix), Arizona, that racial profiling will not be tolerated. Another ruling, involving New York City, will be addressed in the next section. While there are other profiling examples, these two cities represent the problems Latinos, blacks, and other minorities experience with unprofessional law-enforcement agents who fail to abide by the restraints imposed by the Constitution and the courts.

In 2013, U.S. District Court Judge G. Murray Snow concluded in *Melendres v. Arpaio* that Maricopa County Sheriff Arpaio unconstitutionally engaged in racial profiling.[66] The judge found that Arpaio made a concerted effort to target Latinos and impermissibly used race in forming reasonable suspicion of the person's status.[67]

Operations conducted by the Maricopa County Sheriff's Office (MCSO) involved saturation patrols and pretext traffic stops in Latino-populated target areas, resulting in disproportionate stops and arrests.[68] Due to these results, the judge found "circumstantial evidence of discriminatory intent" and barred county officials from detaining, investigating, or arresting Latino vehicle occupants when reasonable suspicion is based only upon a belief or hunch that they are within the country illegally. The judge also prohibited the use of "race or Latino ancestry" as a factor in forming reasonable suspicion to stop a vehicle and the detention of Latino drivers and their passengers longer than reasonably necessary to resolve the traffic violation.[69]

Andrew Cohen, an award-winning journalist, described the *Melendres* anti-profiling opinion as one that provided Arizona and the nation "a great service by chronicling, in meticulous detail, the unconstitutional harassment and racial profiling Hispanic people have been suffering at the hands of Maricopa County Sheriff Joe Arpaio." Judge Snow concluded that Arpaio's well-publicized roundup policies violate both the Fourth Amendment protection against unreasonable seizures, and the Fourteenth Amendment protection against governmental racial and ethnic discrimination.[70] The journalist also commented about the "heavy price paid for the 'success' Sheriff Joe has bragged about for all these years" and the "breathtaking" level of lawlessness that Arpaio routinely engaged in against U.S. Latinos in general and undocumented immigrants in particular. Cohen particularly highlighted MCSO policies that institutionalized the "systematic consideration of race"[71] and resulted in forming the reasonable suspicion or probable cause that led to seizures of Latinos (Cohen 2013).

Based on Arpaio's race-based decisions, the judge concluded that the MCSO violated the Fourteenth Amendment's equal protection clause. Arpaio's deputies continued to consider Latino appearance as probative of a person's lack of immigration status, a practice voided by *Montero-Camargo* and conceded by Arpaio as contrary to law.[72] Arpaio developed a "zero tolerance policy" to justify a claim of a racially neutral plan, but one of his top-ranking officers admitted the policy was specifically designed to "avoid the perception of racial profiling."[73]

Once the Department of Homeland Security (ICE) withdrew Arpaio's authority to operate under 287(g), he publicly asserted that his staff's Internet research convinced him he had independent authority pursuant to the 1996 federal immigration act to enforce unauthorized-presence provisions. Judge Snow found that Arpaio's misunderstanding of the law, aggravated by his failure to rely upon professional legal advice, led to instructions to deputies that placed the rights of minorities in jeopardy.[74]

The federal government indirectly aided Arpaio's political obsession related to aggressive immigration enforcement. ICE provided authority for a maximum of 160 federally trained deputies in 2006.[75] As an elected county sheriff, Arpaio used highly publicized enforcement efforts to garner popular support. In a 2007 press conference announcing the agreement between MCSO and ICE, Arpaio described the "unconstrained" ability "to go after illegals, not the crime first."[76]

The manual used by ICE in training MCSO deputies relied on *Brignoni-Ponce*, even though *Montero-Camargo* in 2000 rejected the broader provision that ethnicity could be one of the factors. *Montero-Camargo* stated that "at minimum, in areas with significant legal Hispanic population, Hispanic descent cannot be a permissible factor in an immigration enforcement context" even if coupled with other factors.[77]

When ICE revoked the MCSO's 287(g) authority,[78] Arpaio created the "LEAR" (Law Enforcement Agency Response Unit) policy, which trained county officers and erroneously reinstated their immigration enforcement authority. LEAR instructed deputies to detain individuals suspected to be in the country illegally but "who cannot be arrested on state charges."[79] According to Judge Snow, the MCSO lost authority to enforce the civil administrative aspects of federal immigration law upon revocation of the 287(g) program. Since mere presence is not a crime, Arpaio's continued alien-detention policy amounted to an unreasonable seizure under the Fourth Amendment.[80]

In 2007, the MCSO announced the beginning of "saturation patrols" involving traffic stops designed to investigate and uncover individuals within the country without authorization.[81] Traffic saturation patrols included the use of Human Smuggling agents positioned in areas where people congregated to find work. Undercover officers would observe a driver pick up a day laborer, and then notify standby patrol units to follow the vehicle until the agents established a basis for a traffic stop.[82] During the stop, which exceeded the concept of a "temporary" detention, the deputy issued a traffic citation while others investigated the immigration status of the passengers.[83] During a four-day operation, the seizure of thirty-five passengers on federal civil violations for undocumented status involved circumstances where the agents lacked prior specific and articulable belief that the detainees were in the country illegally.[84]

Sheriff Arpaio conceded that his office took these day-labor actions to "crack down" on people coming from Mexico.[85] As a result, the judge considered whether the racially based practices violated the Equal Protection Clause of the Fourteenth Amendment.[86] Based on the evidence of race-based enforcement decisions, the judge found an equal protection violation because Arpaio's officers enforced a facially discriminatory policy that considers Latino appearance as probative of a person's lack of authority to be in the United States.[87]

As circumstantial proof of racial animus, the judge noted the testimony of Sgt. Palmer, who admitted that he simply trusted his deputies not to engage in racial profiling. To aggravate matters, Palmer exchanged e-mails that denigrated people of Mexican ancestry and Spanish-speakers with those very deputies he oversaw.[88] After finding that the great majority of Latinos in Maricopa County are citizens, legal residents of the United States, or otherwise authorized aliens, the judge permanently barred the MCSO from using race, or allowing its deputies and other agents to use race, as a criteria in making law enforcement decisions with respect to Latino passengers.[89] He concluded that Latino origin is not a narrowly tailored basis on which one could conclude that the person is an undocumented alien, even if a great majority of those unauthorized persons in Maricopa County are Latino.[90]

In conclusion, the court found that Melendres and his companions were entitled to injunctive relief due to the Fourth and Fourteenth Amendment violations. The judge issued a permanent injunction against Arpaio and the MCSO from (1) detaining Latino occupants of vehicles based only on a reasonable belief that such

persons are in the country without authorization; (2) using race or Latino ancestry as a factor in determining to stop any vehicle in Maricopa County with a Latino occupant, or to detain any Latino occupant to inquire if that person is in the country without authorization; (3) detaining Latino occupants of vehicles stopped for traffic violations for a period longer than reasonably necessary to resolve the traffic violation in the absence of reasonable suspicion that any of them have committed, or are committing, a violation of federal or state criminal law; and (4) detaining Latino occupants of a vehicle for violations of smuggling activity and state employment rules in the absence of a reasonable basis for believing that the necessary elements of the crimes are present.[91] The judge later supplemented his May 2013 opinion by the appointment of a monitor and by entering a final, appealable judgment.[92]

Judge Murray Snow's carefully analyzed opinion in *Melendres v. Arpaio* was not unexpected. For years, Sheriff Arpaio had flaunted his authority. His ostentatious behavior worked well with his predominantly white voters. In his usual populist style, Arpaio immediately and boldly declared his intent to appeal. The ruling should be affirmed. For one, the abundant evidence cited by the judge demonstrates the prevalence of racial profiling of Latinos. Second, the legal authorities relied on are firm. The judge, in distinguishing criminal and civil immigration enforcement, emphasized that in order to enforce federal immigration laws, a local agency must have enforcement authority, a right the MCSO had forfeited.

Arpaio boldly criticized the Department of Homeland Security for questioning his federal immigration enforcement. Appealing to his voters, he promised to continue removal of persons whose appearance indicated their "illegal" status (*New York Times* 2009; Jonsson 2009). After the federal authorities cancelled Maricopa County's 287(g) agreement, Arpaio defiantly declared plans to continue enforcement of state and federal laws (Jonsson 2009). Shortly thereafter, Arpaio announced the arrests of 66 suspects during a weekend sweep, including 30 undocumented persons (Wang 2009). With such a reckless approach to immigration enforcement, Arpaio's deputies predictably seized citizens and resident aliens in the politically obsessive effort to locate immigration violators.

Arpaio continuously expressed that being a day laborer inevitably suggested undocumented status. He also propagated the idea that unauthorized status constituted a crime, and that citizens had a duty to report this "criminal activity." Additionally, the MCSO informed the public of day-labor operations in Latino neighborhoods. Essentially, Arpaio conveyed the perception that illegal immigrants were infiltrating the Latino community, and that citizens should aid law enforcement in removing them and their negative impact on the county's resources.

While *Melendres* prohibits the use of race and fosters the use of race-neutral criteria in making law enforcement decisions, the court order also puts the public on NOTICE that being Latino does not necessarily make one an "illegal." Hopefully, *Melendres* will serve as guidance to police agencies and the public about the impermissibility of using race as an enforcement factor.

New York City's Racially Based Stop-and-Frisk Policy Voided

In *Floyd v. City of New York*, another major racial-profiling ruling, U.S. District Judge Shira Scheindlin found New York Police Department (NYPD) officers violated the Constitution when police targeted minorities with unreasonable stop-and-frisk tactics.[93] After a lengthy non-jury trial, the judge found that NYPD disproportionately targeted people of color by adopting a policy that encouraged police stops of minorities, in minority neighborhoods, to combat crime. More specifically, the judge declared that NYPD "may not target a racially defined group for stops in general—that is, for stops based on suspicions of general criminal wrongdoing—simply because members of that group appear frequently in the police department's suspect data."[94]

Judge Scheindlin found violations of the Fourth Amendment's ban on unreasonable searches and the Fourteenth Amendment's equal protection clause (Weiss 2013b).[95] As to the equal protection claim, the judge said that plaintiffs had to establish that discriminatory purpose was a motivating factor, although it did not necessarily have to be the sole or predominant factor in a police enforcement action. Interestingly, questions surrounding a police officer's motives are irrelevant in Fourth Amendment claims, but proof of a discriminatory motive is essential in proving a Fourteenth Amendment violation.[96]

In explaining her ruling, the judge highlighted the importance of recognizing "the human toll of unconstitutional stops," but further recognized that, even though a police detention is a "limited intrusion in duration and deprivation of liberty," each stop also constitutes a "demeaning and humiliating experience."[97] The court found that those subjected to routine stops are "overwhelmingly" minorities who are "troubled to be singled out when many of them have done nothing to attract the unwanted attention."[98] These comments derived from the judge's review of statistics on 4.4 million police stops during an eight-year period. Of these, at least 200,000 stops, about 6 percent, lacked the constitutional reasonable suspicion required by the Fourth Amendment.[99]

The judge also heard evidence of an unwritten policy of the NYPD to target "the right people" for stops.[100] She found this to be "a form of racial profiling" since not all members of a racially defined group should be subjected to heightened police enforcement because some members of that group are criminals.[101] According to *Floyd*, 52 percent of NYPD stops were followed by a frisk for weapons, yet only 1.5 percent of those frisks resulted in a police discovery of a weapon. In other words, in 98.5 percent of the protective frisks, the people did not possess a weapon.[102]

In 52 percent of the stops, the person stopped was black; in 31 percent, Latino; and in 10 percent, white. In these street encounters, police seized weapons in 1 percent of the stops of blacks; 1.1 percent, Latinos; and 1.4 percent, whites. Similarly, the police seized contraband other than weapons in 1.8 percent of the stops of blacks; 1.7 percent, Latinos; and 2.3 percent, whites.[103]

Whren v. United States[104] figured prominently in Judge Scheindlin's analysis. The opinion involved an encounter similar to a "vehicular stop-and-frisk." The accused challenged a Washington, DC, police practice of patrolling "high drug" neighborhoods in unmarked cars and stopping drivers for minor traffic violations. The officers stopped Whren and his companion for speeding. When the officer approached the driver, he observed bags of crack cocaine in plain view in the passenger's hands.[105] The defense claimed the stop was pretextual, but the Court decided that the reason for the stop was irrelevant, adding that the objective reasonableness of the stop determined the outcome for Fourth Amendment purposes. Justice Scalia, for the Court, added that a "selective enforcement" claim based on race must be established under Equal Protection Clause jurisprudence.[106]

In *Floyd*, the judge ordered that a stop-and-frisk be conducted in a "racially neutral manner."[107] She added that overwhelming proof existed that "the city's highest officials have turned a blind eye to the evidence that officers are conducting stops in a racially discriminatory manner,"[108] a reference that likely included former mayor Michael Bloomberg, a proponent of aggressive policing. Another top official included the NYPD police commissioner. Senator Eric Adams, a former NYPD captain, testified that he attended a meeting where police commissioner Raymond Kelly recommended stopping racially defined groups just to instill fear in those communities. Kelly's comments responded to concerns raised by Adams about the disproportionate number of blacks and Hispanics who had been targeted.[109] Commissioner Kelly responded that he focused on young blacks and Hispanics since they should know that "every time they leave their home, they could be stopped by the police."[110] Kelly declined to appear at trial to rebut these claims. His inflexible stance angered many, including college students at an Ivy League school who heckled him when he appeared to speak on proactive policing (Pearce 2013).

Cornell law professor Sherry F. Colb reviewed the district court's comprehensive *Floyd* opinion. Professor Colb noted the quite persuasive extent of the district judge's findings, which included determinations that New York City police, with approval from superiors, regularly performed stop-and-frisks in the absence of reasonable suspicion, even if they lacked indications that the targets were armed and presently dangerous. Colb's analysis of racial profiling includes a discussion as to whether the underlying motivation is a feeling of hatred for people in the targeted group, or whether it instead involves the sincere belief that members of that group commit crimes at a disproportionate rate. In other words, the important factor is that "race or ethnicity plays a role in the decision, not the officer's reason for making decisions" (Colb 2013).[111]

Shortly after the *Floyd* ruling, the people of New York City overwhelmingly elected a mayor who vowed to change these discriminatory stop-and-frisk practices. Since the *Floyd* plaintiffs requested only an injunction and not monetary damages, it is unlikely that there will be any real chance for appellate review at the Supreme Court unless the Second Circuit reverses the district judge's lengthy and well-documented case.[112] The parties requested a stay of appellate proceedings so that they could discuss settlement possibilities.

NOTES

1. U.S. Const. amend. V.

2. U.S. Const. amend. XIV, § 1.

3. Yick Wo v. Hopkins, 118 U.S. 356 (1886).

4. Arizona v. United States, 132 S. Ct. 2492 (2012); United States v. Alabama, 691 F.3d 1269, 1280–81 (11th Cir. 2012).

5. Mora v. Arpaio, No. CV-09–1719-PHX-DGC, 2011 U.S. Dist. LEXIS 45098, at 1–2 (D. Ariz. Apr. 25, 2011).

6. Ibid.

7. Terry v. Ohio, 392 U.S. 1, 21 (1968).

8. Mora, 2011 U.S. Dist. LEXIS 45098, at 29–30.

9. Melendres v. Arpaio, 989 F. Supp. 2d 822, 2013 U.S. Dist. LEXIS 73869, at 216 (D. Ariz. May 24, 2013); Melendres v. Arpaio, 695 F.3d 990, 1000 (9th Cir. 2012), where the Ninth Circuit Court of Appeals concluded that the Latino litigants were likely to succeed in their claim that the Fourth Amendment does not permit a stop or detention based solely on unlawful presence.

10. U.S. CONST. amend. IV; United States v. Otherson, 637 F.2d 1276 (9th Cir. 1980).

11. The two statutes are the Antiterrorism and Effective Death Penalty Act (AEDPA), Pub. L. 104–142, § 401–443, 110 Stat. 1214, 1258–81 (1996), codified at 18 U.S.C. § 2339B (a) (7)

(2006), and the Illegal Immigration Reform and Immigrant Responsibility Act (IIRIRA), Pub. L. 104–208, Div. C, 110 Stat. at 3009–546 through 3009–724 (1996), 8 U.S.C. § 1101 *et seq.* (2006). They extensively amended the Immigration and Nationality Act of 1952 (INA), 66 Stat. 163 (1952).

12. 8 U.S.C. § 1357(g) (5) (2006).

13. Ibid., (g) (1), (g) (2).

14. Ibid., (g) (10).

15. Pursuant to 42 U.S.C. § 14141, the United States is authorized to sue a state or local government for equitable and declaratory relief when that government engages in a pattern or practice of conduct by law enforcement officers that deprives persons of rights secured by the Constitution or laws of the United States.

16. Terry, 392 U.S. at 1, 27.

17. Ibid., 21.

18. Ibid., 27.

19. Whren v. United States, 517 U.S. 806 (1996).

20. Ibid., 808.

21. Ibid.

22. Ibid., 808–09.

23. Ibid., 809.

24. Ibid., 810.

25. Ibid.

26. Ibid., 810–11.

27. United States v. Brignoni-Ponce, 422 U.S. 873, 876 (1975).

28. Ibid., 884.

29. Ibid., 882.

30. Ibid.

31. United States v. Broomfield, 417 F.3d 654, 655 (7th Cir. 2005).

32. United States v. Brignoni-Ponce, 422 U.S. 873, 886–87 (1975).

33. See Terry v. Ohio, 392 U.S. 1, 10–11 (1968).

34. Brignoni-Ponce, 422 U.S. at 882.

35. See 8 U.S.C. § 1357(g) (2006).

36. Brignoni-Ponce, 422 U.S. at 884–85.

37. Ibid., 885.

38. Ibid.

39. United States v. Zapata-Ibarra, 212 F.3d 877, 885 (5th Cir. 2000); 223 F.3d 281 (5th Cir. 2000) (Wiener J., dissenting).

40. United States v. Zapata-Ibarra, 223 F.3d 281, 282 (5th Cir. 2000).

41. Ibid., 281.

42. Ibid.

43. *E.g.*, Korematsu v. United States, 323 U.S. 214, 215–16 (1944) (Japanese Internment Case during World War II).

44. Zapata-Ibarra, 223 F.3d at 282.

45. Ibid.

46. Ibid., 282–83 (footnotes omitted).

47. Ibid., 284.

48. Ibid.

49. Ibid., 285.

50. Ibid.

51. United States v. Montero-Camargo, 208 F.3d 1122, 1133 (9th Cir.) (en banc). Eleven members of the Ninth Circuit participated in the decision.

52. Ibid., 1134.

53. Sanchez-Guillen v. United States, 531 U.S. 889 (2000).

54. The Ninth Circuit states include Alaska, Arizona, California, Hawaii, Idaho, Montana, Nevada, Oregon, and Washington, four states with sizable Latino populations.

55. United States v. Montero-Camargo, 208 F.3d 1122, 1128 (9th Cir. 2000) (en banc).

56. Ibid.

57. Ibid., 1128–29.

58. Ibid., 1132.

59. Ibid.

60. United States v. Brignoni-Ponce, 422 U.S. 873, 886 n. 12 (1975).

61. Montero-Camargo, 208 F.3d at 1132–33.

62. 132 S. Ct. 2492 (2012).

63. Ibid., 2501–06.

64. 132 S. Ct. at 2509.

65. Ibid., 2510.

66. Melendres v. Arpaio, 989 F. Supp. 2d 822, 2013 U.S. Dist. LEXIS 73869, at 139–40 (D. Ariz. May 24, 2013).

67. Ibid., 258–59.

68. Ibid., 139–40.

69. Ibid., 273–74.

70. Ibid., 273–74.

71. Ibid., 233.

72. Ibid., 10, 224, 230, 233–34.

73. Ibid., 245.

74. Ibid., 250.

75. Ibid., 5. The federal-local agreement, known as the 287(g) program, derives from the Immigration and Nationality Act, § 287 (g), codified at 8 U.S.C. § 1357 (g).

76. Ibid., 22.

77. Ibid., 227–31.

78. Ibid., 6.

79. Ibid., 9–10.

80. Ibid., 6–7.

81. Ibid., 23–24.

82. United States v. Broomfield, 417 F.3d 654, 655 (7th Cir. 2005).

83. Melendres v. Arpaio, 989 F. Supp. 2d 822, 2013 U.S. Dist. LEXIS 73869, at 24 (D. Ariz. May 24, 2013).

84. Ibid., 25.

85. Ibid., 26.

86. Ibid., 233–34.

87. Ibid., 234.

88. Ibid., 242.

89. Ibid., 254.

90. Ibid., 240.

91. Ibid., 269–70.

92. Melendres v. Arpaio, 989 F. Supp. 2d 822, 2013 U.S. Dist. LEXIS 145859, at 80–100 (D. Ariz. Oct. 2, 2013).

93. Floyd v. City of New York, 959 F. Supp. 2d 540 (S.D.N.Y. 2013).

94. Ibid., 563.

95. Ibid., 660–61, 662–64.

96. Whren v. United States, 517 U.S. 806, 813 (1996).

97. Floyd v. City of New York, 959 F. Supp. 2d 540, 557 (S.D.N.Y. 2013).

98. Ibid.

99. Ibid., 559.

100. Ibid., 560.

101. Ibid., 561.

102. Ibid., 573.

103. Ibid., 574.

104. Whren v. United States, 517 U.S. 806 (1996).

105. Ibid., 808–09.

106. Ibid., 813.

107. Floyd v. City of New York, 959 F. Supp. 2d 540, 556 (S.D.N.Y. 2013).

108. Ibid., 562.

109. Ibid., 606.

110. Ibid.

111. In *Washington v. Davis*, 426 U.S. 229, 239 (1976), the Court found an exam for potential police candidates was not purposely prepared as a mechanism for discriminating against African American applicants.

112. The district court opinion contains 783 footnotes. The appeal from her order was docketed in the Court of Appeals for the Second Circuit. Ligon v. City of New York, 743 F.3d 362 (2nd Cir. 2014).

REFERENCES

ACLU. 2005. "Racial Profiling: Definition." November 23. http://www.aclu.org/racial-justice/racial-profiling-definition.

ACLU. 2011. "ACLU, Maricopa County Reach Settlement in Lawsuit by U.S. Citizen, Legal Resident Illegally Arrested during Worksite Raid." News release. July 7. http://acluaz.org/issues/racial-justice/2011-07/991.

ACLU. 2011. "Joe Arpaio Loses Again: Maricopa County Settles for $200K in Mora Racial-Profiling Case." *Phoenix New Times*, July 7. http://blogs.phoenixnewtimes.com/bastard/2011/07/joe_arpaio_loses_again_maricop.php

Balderrama, Francisco E., and Raymond Rodriguez. 1995. *Decade of Betrayal: Mexican Repatriation in the 1930s*. Albuquerque: University of New Mexico Press.

BBVM. 2009. "Sheriff Arpaio Slapped with Another Civil Rights Lawsuit over Arrests." *Big Bear Observation Post* (blog), August 21. http://bbvm.wordpress.com/2009/08/21/sheriff-arpaio-slapped-with-another-civil-rights-lawsuit-over-arrests/.

Bender, Steven W., Raquel Aldana, Gilbert P. Carrasco, and Joaquin G. Avila. 2008. *Everyday Law for Latino/as*. Boulder, CO: Paradigm Publishers.

Carroll, Susan. 2010. "Man Born at Ben Taub Returns after He's Wrongly Deported." *Houston Chronicle*, September 14.

Cohen, Andrew. 2013. "Federal Judge Chronicles Lawlessness of Joe Arpaio–Led Sheriff's Office." *Atlantic*, May 25.

Colb, Sherry F. 2013. "A Federal Court Holds New York Stop-and-Frisk Policy Unconstitutional in Floyd v. City of New York." August 21. http://verdict.justia.com/2013/08/21/a-federal-court-holds-new-york-stop-and-frisk-policy-unconstitutional-in-floyd-v-city-of-new-york.

Fox News Latino. 2013. "Racial Profiling of Latinos in North Carolina County Confirmed by Justice Department Study." December 6. http://latino.foxnews.com/latino/news/2013/12/06/racial-profiling-latinos-in-north-carolina-county-confirmed-by-justice/.

Gardner II, Trevor, and Aarti Kohli. 2009. "The C.A.P. Effect: Racial Profiling in the ICE Criminal Alien Program." September. http://www.law.berkeley.edu/files/policybrief_irving_final.pdf.

Gowie, Renata Ann. 2001. "Driving While Mexican: Why the Supreme Court Must Reexamine United States v. Brignoni-Ponce, 422 U.S. 873 (1975)." *Houston Journal of International Law* 23: 233–52.

Harris, David A. 2002. *Profiles in Injustice: Why Racial Profiling Cannot Work*. New York: New Press.

Johnson, Kevin R. 2010. "How Racial Profiling in America Became the Law of the Land: United States v. Brignoni-Ponce and Whren v. United States and the Need for Truly Rebellious Lawyering." *Georgetown Law Journal* 98: 1005–77.

Jonsson, Patrik. 2009. "Sheriff Joe Arpaio: I Don't Take Orders from Anybody: Refusal by 'America's Toughest Sheriff' to Stop Immigration Sweeps Fits into the Career of a Controversial Populist." *Christian Science Monitor*, October 17.

Kitchen, S. C., Turrentine Law Firm. 2012. Letter to Thomas E. Perez, Assistant Attorney General, U.S. Department of Justice, Civil Rights Division. September 26. http://triad.johnlocke.org/blog/wp-content/uploads/2012/09/johnson.pdf.

Lemons, Stephen. 2009. "He Never Flinched: A U.S. Citizen Was Detained by the MCSO and Then Testified before Congress about His Being Racially Profiled." *Phoenix New Times*, December 3.

Mears, Bill. 2011. "Obama Administration Asks Court to Block Parts of Tough Alabama Immigration Law." *CNN*, October 7.

New York Times. 2009. "Wrong Paths to Immigration Reform." Editorial. October 12.

Passel, Jeffrey S., D'Vera Cohn, and Mark Hugo Lopez. 2011. "Census 2010: 50 Million Latinos, Hispanics Account for More Than Half of Nation's Growth in Past Decade." *Pew Hispanic Center*, March 24. http://pewhispanic.org/files/reports/140.pdf.

Pearce, Matt. 2013. "NYPD's Raymond Kelly Walks out of Brown University Talk after Heckling." *Los Angeles Times*, October 30.

Perez, Thomas E., Assistant Attorney General, U.S. Department of Justice, Civil Rights Division. 2012.

Letter to Clyde Albright, County Attorney for Alamance County and Chuck Kitchen, Turrentine Law Firm, Re: United States' Investigation of the Alamance County Sheriff's Office. September 18.

Pham, Huyen. 2004. "The Inherent Flaws in the Inherent Authority Position: Why Inviting Local Enforcement of Immigration Laws Violates the Constitution." *Florida State University Law Review* 31: 965–1003.

Perez, Thomas E., Assistant Attorney General, U.S. Department of Justice, Civil Rights Division.. 2012b. "Incidents and Offenses." December. http://www.fbi.gov/about-us/cjis/ucr/hate-crime/2011/narratives/incidentsandoffenses_final.pdf.

Pitt, Leonard. 1966. *The Decline of the Californios: A Social History of the Spanish-speaking Californians, 1846–1890.* Berkeley: University of California Press.

Pruitt, Lisa R. 2009. "Latina/os, Locality, and Law in the Rural South." *Harvard Latino Law Review* 12: 135–69.

Rodriguez, Juan C. 2009. "Study: Hispanics Wary of Cops, Courts." *Albuquerque Journal*, April 8.

Romero, Mary, and Marwah Serag. 2005. "Violation of Latino Civil Rights Resulting from INS and Local Police's Use of Race, Culture and Class Profiling: The Case of the Chandler Roundup in Arizona." *Cleveland State Law Review* 52: 75–96.

Romero, Victor C. 2000. "Racial Profiling: Driving While Mexican and Affirmative Action." *Michigan Journal of Race & Law* 6: 195–207.

Rubin, Paul. 2008. "Judge Jose Padilla Says He Was Racially Profiled Twice before Traffic Stops." *Phoenix New Times*, July 24.

Ruiz, Albor. 2009. "President Obama, Please Don't Expand Failed Immigration Program 287(g)." *New York Daily News*, July 18.

Salinas, Guadalupe, and Isaias D. Torres. 1976. "The Undocumented Mexican Alien: A Legal, Social and Economic Analysis." *Houston Law Review* 13: 863–916.

Salinas, Lupe S., and Fernando Colon-Navarro. 2011. "Racial Profiling as a Means of Thwarting the Alleged Latino Security Threat." *Thurgood Marshall Law Review* 37: 5–44.

Stelter, Brian, and Bill Carter. 2009. "Lou Dobbs Abruptly Quits CNN." *New York Times*, November 11.

U.S. Department of Homeland Security. 2009. "ICE Announces Standardized 287(g) Agreements with 67 State and Local Law Enforcement Partners." News release. October 16. http://www.ICE.gov/news/releases/0910/091016washingtondc.htm.

U.S. Department of Justice. 1996. "Assistance by State and Local Police in Apprehending Illegal Aliens." February 5. http://www.justice.gov/olc/immstop01.htm.

Valencia, Nick. 2011. "My Encounter with Anti-Latino Racism." Editorial. *CNN Opinion*, September 29.

Vargas, Sylvia R. 2002. "Missouri, the 'War on Terrorism,' and Immigrants: Legal Challenges Post 9/11." *Missouri Law Review* 67: 775–830.

Wang, Amy B. 2009. "Weekend Sweep Nets 66 Arrests, Sheriff Says." *Arizona Republic*, October 20.

Weiss, Debra Cassens. 2013b. "Stop-and-Frisk Tactics by New York Cops Violated Fourth and 14th Amendments, Judge Rules." *ABA Journal*, August 12.

Weissman, Deborah M., Director of Clinical Programs, University of North Carolina at Chapel Hill School of Law. 2009. "State and Local Enforcement of Immigration Laws." Statement before the Committee on House Judiciary, Subcommittee on Constitution, Civil Rights, and Civil Liberties. *Congressional Quarterly*, April.

Weissman, Deborah M., Rebecca C. Headen, and Katherine Lewis Parker. 2009. "The Policies and Politics of Local Immigration Enforcement Laws: 287(g) Program in North Carolina." February. http://www.law.unc.edu/documents/clinicalprograms/287gpolicyreview.pdf.

Ye Hee Lee, Michelle. 2012. "Maricopa County Feuds Cost Taxpayers $28 Million." *AZ Central*, June 18.

Ye Hee Lee, Michelle, and Michael Kiefer. 2013. "Maricopa County Supervisors Settle Lawsuits Filed by 'New Times' Founders, Stapley." *AZ Central*, December 20.

Framing Immigration

"Illegality" and the Role of Political Communication

Natalie Masuoka and Jane Junn

During the 1994 California gubernatorial race, Republican Pete Wilson sought to revive what appeared to be a failing bid for reelection by taking a tough stance against illegal immigration. Ironically, when Wilson was a US senator from California, he had fought to preserve farmers' easy access to immigrant labor during congressional deliberation on the 1986 Immigration Reform and Control Act (Newton 2008). In 1994, however, amid growing public concern over rising levels of immigration, Wilson supported the ballot initiative Proposition 187, which would deny public services to unauthorized immigrants, including public-school education for children. To mobilize voter support for his reelection, Wilson ran television advertisements highlighting immigration. One of the ads showed a grainy video of people running across the US-Mexico border checkpoint with the ominous voice-over "They keep coming." Political communications such as these and Governor Wilson's support of Proposition 187 have been argued to have been important factors in his successful reelection (Nicholson 2005).

As concern over immigration has moved onto the national agenda, political candidates across the country are expected to take positions on immigration. In 2008 immigration was considered a powerful issue to mobilize voters, so much so that most candidates vying for their party's nomination, including then senator Barack Obama, made immigration a core policy issue. Colorado congressman Tom Tancredo centered his bid for the Republican nomination on the issue of immigration and border security. In a campaign advertisement later dubbed "Someone Needs to Say It," the self-described "border hawk" linked immigration and terrorism.[1] In this ad, a hooded figure with a backpack is seen walking, with the sound of a clock ticking loudly in the background. The ad ends with a black screen reading, "Before it's too late," accompanied by the sound of a bomb exploding.

In this chapter, we consider how public opinion on immigration is influenced by political elites and political communication. How competing candidates frame issues and the images they use to prime voters can drastically change the contours of debate over policy. Political campaigns are in many ways battles over creating the most convincing message (Chong and Druckman 2007). Political scientists know that individuals' attitudes on issues are based on their experiences and personal predispositions, but people are also systematically influenced by political communications. To motivate fear or threat, politicians can make linkages between immigration and national security. Alternatively, activists can emphasize fairness and opportunity in order to mobilize support for more open immigration policies. Individual attitudes toward immigration policy can be strongly influenced by competing messages that encourage individuals to prioritize some values over others.

In the contemporary debate over immigration policy reform, two characteristics of immigrants are often highlighted: residency status and racial background. Concerns about these issues are not new to the nation, and they continue to stir controversy in American politics. Unauthorized immigration has been identified as a national problem ever since the United States began placing numeric quotas on the number of immigrants allowed into the country, starting with the 1882 Chinese Exclusion Act (Ngai 2004). Moreover, the process of racial othering has been applied to all waves of immigrants, including those from southern and eastern Europe in the early twentieth century (M. Jacobson 1999; Roediger 2005). In particular, these two factors have been hypothesized to mobilize restrictive attitudes toward immigration, as they are assumed to challenge American assumptions about national membership and belonging (Brader, Valentino, and Suhay 2006; Burns

and Gimpel 2000; Nevins 2002; Ngai 2004). However, the view that illegal residence and nonwhite race are perceived as a violation of American values presumes that all Americans hold the same assumptions about national belonging. Based on the evidence presented the foregoing chapters, we posit that racial groups will respond very differently to political messages on immigration policy.

The evidence presented in this chapter shows that whites and racial minorities do respond to messages that highlight illegality or race in systematically different ways. This further demonstrates how consequential the racial hierarchy is in individual attitude formation. The racial hierarchy leads members of racial groups to develop their own views and assumptions about membership in the United States polity. Because racial groups differ in their baseline assumptions, the relevant considerations that are triggered by a political appeal will vary systematically. We thus cannot assume that a given political message will activate consistent responses across groups. In order to make reliable predictions of how a political communication strategy will work, social-scientific theories must first acknowledge how the racial hierarchy structures the baseline assumptions that are implicitly communicated in a political appeal. Theories on the role of political communication must provide a more exact match between the message of the political appeal and who constitutes the targeted audience.

Communication Strategies and the Formation of Public Opinion

In our everyday lives we witness how others make firm decisions or confidently express an opinion about a particular event. In this way, we expect a person's political attitudes to reflect a clear and consistent set of preferences. However, as any review of American elections would suggest, American preferences can change. Political leaders, public laws, and governing processes change with shifts in American attitudes. Political scientists know that, in reality, individual opinion about a political issue is malleable. This is because an individual's political position on an issue is often influenced by external sources of information or by a convincing

argument. As John Zaller (1992) explains, there are two important components to attitude formation: the "information to form a mental picture of the given issue, and predisposition to motivate some conclusion about it" (6). This perspective leads us, on the one hand, to be optimistic about the human capacity to learn and compromise: political attitudes can change for the better when there is new information that leads a person to reconsider his or her position. However, on the other hand, it also means that opinion can be shaped by a convincing message that has been strategically developed to generate support for a particular political cause. It is in reference to this second perspective that we develop the ideas in this chapter.

"Politics in a democratic society," as succinctly described by Sniderman and Theriault (2004), "is distinctively the domain in which choices are contestable legitimately ... [and] political preferences are contestable because choices necessarily must be made between competing values" (140). All public policies, including issues related to immigration, can generate competing interests. Some individuals see that they may benefit from a new policy, and others will immediately see what they can lose. Since governing decisions ultimately require the support of the public, competing interest groups, political parties, and elected officials all engage in political campaigns to generate support among voters for their own position. Because of this, the public is exposed to many different ways of looking at a policy. Because voters are not experts on every proposed policy, messages produced to mobilize support for a particular position can strongly influence individual opinion formation.

In general, scholars have identified two primary communications strategies employed by political elites and the media to mold public opinion, which have been labeled as "framing" and "priming." The distinction between framing and priming is subtle but important. Politicians employ framing by emphasizing those values or perceptions deemed most important to evaluating a policy (Druckman 2010). An issue frame is powerful because it provides "a central organizing idea or story line that provides meaning to an unfolding strip of events, weaving a connection among them. The frame suggests what the controversy is about, the essence of the issue" (Gamson and Modigliani 1987, 143). Framing is a useful tool for political elites because it helps direct focus to a particular value that makes a particular position more compelling. A common frame in today's immigration debate is the emphasis on "illegal" immigration. As we outline below, by emphasizing the distinction between "legal" and "illegal," politicians direct attention to the values of fairness, importance of law, and protection of national identity as justification for more punitive immigration policies.

Priming, on the other hand, occurs when politicians or media call "attention to some matters while ignoring others" (Kinder and Iyengar 1989, 63; see also Valentino 1999). Priming encourages individuals to think of certain characteristics or attributes as more relevant than others. Priming is often most powerful because it can activate what is considered implicit thinking or the more subtle and sometimes subconscious thoughts held by individuals. Social characteristics are connected to certain values, ideas, or emotions (Conover 1984). When an individual is primed to think about a particular characteristic, certain responses are also activated, such as positive or negative affect or an emotional response such as fear. Through priming, elites can activate predictable responses by emphasizing characteristics that they know will generate other implicit responses. To be sure, there are many individual-level characteristics such as age or occupation that affect Americans' evaluation of immigrants. However, immigrants' racial background is arguably more politically consequential to the formation of attitudes about immigration, given the controversies and tensions surrounding race in the United States. By providing cues evoking immigrants' racial background, politicians seek to make race one of the first considerations the public relies upon when making decisions about immigration policy.

Although framing and priming are distinct processes, evidence has found that both have similar effects on the formation of political attitudes in that they do become incorporated into how individuals think and talk about issues. Studies on framing show that people will adopt and employ frames presented by political elites (Gamson 1992; Druckman and Nelson 2003; Druckman et al. 2010). Gamson and Modigliani's (1987) study on affirmative action shows that frames emphasizing undeserved advantage and reverse discrimination today are commonly used to reject the policy. Furthermore, the classic study on the media by Iyengar and Kinder (1987) shows close correspondence between issues primed by the media and issues listed by viewers as extremely important. Recent studies also confirm that in addition to influencing the public's stance on an issue, politicians can also mobilize emotions, predispositions, or concerns through the use of priming. For example, research on implicit racial appeals show that white racial resentment is activated when whites are exposed to political appeals that prime the audience to think about blacks (Mendelberg 2001; Henry and Sears 2002).[2]

The Racial Hierarchy and Political Appeals

While the influence of framing and priming on the formation of public opinion is well documented, the reliability of framing and priming effects across the entire voting public has come into question. One of the perceived strengths of framing and priming is the ability of both strategies to influence attitudes across the electorate in predictable directions. Evidence tells us, however, that racial groups vary in their responses to political appeals. One reason differences in the effect of framing and priming on different races have been overlooked is that these communication strategies are traditionally assumed to function at a basic cognitive level by constraining the possible choices made available to individuals. As such, variation in how individuals respond to framing and priming is explained primarily by theories of cognition. But what is often overlooked is that the choices offered by these strategies are strongly informed by political culture and surrounding context. How a respondent chooses to interpret those choices is thus not only a matter of cognition but is also influenced by the cultural assumptions highlighted by a political appeal. This is most apparent in cross-national comparisons. As a simple example, say a message alludes to party competition. In the United States, Americans will automatically refer to their two-party system. In contrast, Western Europeans will likely assume a more complex multiparty system.

Thus, even if all cognitive factors are held constant, individuals from different groups may systematically respond differently to a political message because they hold different assumptions about their social world. These assumptions lead individuals to interpret the intent of a political message in unique ways. Individuals' assumptions vary because they exist in different contexts. This means that, aside from cognition, another key factor that moderates how individuals respond to framing and priming is social context. But while context is widely recognized to vary across nations, we argue that social hierarchies also lead members of the same nation to occupy unique contexts (see Philpot and White 2010). When individuals are ordered along a social hierarchy, social status determines how each person experiences social interactions

and other processes. Indeed, in previous chapters we demonstrate the systematically distinct assumptions each racial group holds. The context informed by each group's placement in the racial hierarchy strongly informs perceptions of national membership and group identity. Placement in the hierarchy also informs how groups view others. Our analysis of stereotyping shows that in-group favoritism is exercised the strongest by those ranked at the top of the hierarchy.

Although we may expect racial groups to respond differently to communication strategies, studies testing the varying effects of framing and priming across racial groups are limited in number. Most studies in both political science and psychology test only white respondents. However, Ismail White's (2007) analysis of the different effects of racial appeals on white and black respondents is particularly informative about the moderating role of the racial hierarchy.[3] Racial appeals include political strategies that employ "the race card" and messages that highlight racial differences in order to generate perceptions of threat. However, as White indicates, racial appeals primarily highlight the deficiencies of blacks with the intent of generating white racial resentment. White's experimental tests showed that explicit racial appeals that directly connected blacks with a political issue were found to activate positive in-group identification among black respondents. But, consistent with previous findings, White found that implicit racial appeals activated racial resentment among whites.

These opposing results between white and black respondents found by White encourage us to develop two important perspectives for developing a more detailed theory about the effects of framing and priming. First, before generating hypotheses about the effects of a message, scholars must pay attention to the intended audience of the message. Political elites and the media generate communication strategies to mobilize particular groups. Political appeals attempt to tap into deeply held assumptions and values of the targeted audience. Second, scholars must be aware that, because racial groups hold different assumptions about how society operates, a political appeal may have the unintended effect of mobilizing the opposite response among racial populations other than the targeted group. These unintended effects may have severe political consequences. Take, for example, the political landscape of California, which is now a majority "minority" population. While Wilson's 1994 advertisements described in the introduction of this chapter worked as expected on the native-born white electorate, they were interpreted quite differently by the Latino population. Latinos became staunchly Democratic in the state after 1994, and the California Republican Party has been unable to reverse that trend since. Today, Latinos make up nearly one-third of the California population, which may further doom Republican political power in the state (Pantoja, Ramirez, and Segura 2001).

We should expect there to be differences in framing and priming effects on different races in some instances but not all. It is not an inherent rule that racial groups will respond differently to political messages. White's attention to racial appeals was purposeful because the particular values and assumptions highlighted in racial appeals represent those that will cause racial-group responses to diverge. Racial appeals work because they imply to the targeted audience that certain groups are deviating from what are considered important values and behaviors. But while the values and behaviors held in esteem by one group might be assumed to be shared by all, they are in reality strongly affected by the racial hierarchy. The racial hierarchy informs the desirability of many values and behaviors. Behaviors understood to be socially desirable are assumed to be practiced by the dominant group in the racial hierarchy. For example, laziness is assumed to be a trait of low-ranked groups in the hierarchy, while hard work is an assumed trait of those ranked at the top of the hierarchy. Secondly, many of the most esteemed American norms, such as individualism, disregard the existence of a racial hierarchy. These norms tend to assume that there is equality in individual agency. Personal success, for example, is assumed to be a direct result of self-sufficiency and industriousness because there are no identified structural barriers that restrain action. This is true for those ranked at the top of the hierarchy, but for those ranked at the bottom of the racial hierarchy, individual lives are heavily structured. So while individualism may be perceived as important,

racial minorities personally witness that it does not apply equally to all. Those who recognize the inequalities that exist in these norms are less likely to feel threatened or disappointed if those norms are violated.

Therefore, to understand the influence of political messages on individual attitude formation, we must recognize the role of racial hierarchy on both sides of communication. In messages employed by elites to mold public opinion, we find that the structure of the racial hierarchy is strongly implied in the content of a message. Elites often attempt to mobilize feelings of outrage, resentment, or threat by highlighting how a certain group violates cherished values embraced by the target audience. However, those implied norms are often used to uphold the existing social hierarchy. We must remember that political communications serve strategic purposes, and political elites draft their messages so that they resonate most among the target audience. Often the target audience is not the entire public but a very specific subpopulation. On the receiving end of the message, the racial hierarchy informs individuals' perceptions about society and politics. A political message will be consumed differently by each racial group because each group's perspective is structured by that group's position in the racial order.

As the examples in the introduction of this chapter suggest, framing and priming are often used to mobilize restrictive responses to immigration. In the remainder of this chapter, we examine two common communications strategies that have been employed in recent years: framing immigrants as "illegal" as opposed to "legal" and priming respondents to pay attention to the (nonwhite) racial background of new immigrants. Each strategy is assumed to have strong and predictable effects on mobilizing negative attitudes toward immigrants. Narratives that emphasize illegality in their framing direct attention away from considering immigrants as productive and desirable new members of the nation and toward thinking about immigrants as criminals. Illegal immigrants are presented as individuals who violate American norms of what is fair and lawful. As an example of priming, highlighting the nonwhite backgrounds of new immigrants is a strategy used to activate ethnocentrism or racism. By priming respondents to think of immigrants as nonwhite, political appeals remind respondents that they are inherently different and of an undesirable race.

In the two studies described below, we aim to demonstrate that political messages intended to generate restrictive attitudes toward immigration are not effective for influencing the opinion of all racial groups. We posit that communication strategies that seek to mobilize restrictive attitudes about immigration are explicitly lobbying for maintenance of the status quo. Immigrants cause changes to existing society that are perceived to be undesirable. To tap into this, communication strategies highlight why or how immigrants change society by implicating the racial hierarchy. Therefore, we expect to find that the group who enjoys the most benefits from that hierarchy, whites, are those most easily influenced by these strategies. White respondents will report more restrictive attitudes toward immigration in response to frames of illegality and to racial priming. In contrast, racial minorities, whose status remains marginalized because of the hierarchy, are all less subject to these strategies.

Framing: Examining Differences in Attitudes toward "Illegal" Immigration

The choice to use the term "illegal" to frame those immigrants who arrive without visas is an explicit political attempt to conjure specific norms of fairness, legal justice, and equality (Nevins 2002).[4] These norms at first glance may appear to be universally desirable and race-neutral values. If all Americans are assumed to value these norms, then the illegal-immigration frame could be expected to effectively mobilize restrictive immigration attitudes among all Americans, regardless of their race. However, the assumption that American law has been and continues to be color-blind is far from the truth. Legal historians have long pointed out that preferences to maintain white supremacy serve as clear motivations in codified law. Examples ranging from the early framers' decision to continue slavery to the modern legal decisions upholding racial segregation demonstrate how the law has not equally protected all Americans. Like other sectors of law, immigration policy and rules governing entry and abode have been created to help maintain the racial hierarchy in the United States. Before turning to our analysis of survey data, we first review how "illegality" has been constructed in the United States. This review will help inform our expectations of how racial groups will react to frames emphasizing illegal immigration.

The Construction of the "Illegal Alien"

The legal-illegal distinction is a relatively modern one for Americans. It began when the US government first placed quotas on the number of immigrants entering the country after the 1924 National Origins Act.[5] Over the last century, the distinction between legal and illegal immigration has arguably become a dominant one in the minds of Americans. Public outcry against illegal immigration is thought to have peaked in the early 1990s (Newton 2008). It was in this period that the federal government began to implement new policies targeting illegal immigration such as Operation Gatekeeper in 1994 and the Illegal Immigration Reform and Immigrant Responsibility Act in 1996. In this cultural movement toward a legal-illegal distinction, legal immigrants are often assumed to be an acceptable and welcomed subset of immigrants. Legal immigrants are "lawful" residents because they were officially authorized to enter the country. Illegal immigrants are "lawbreakers" who have entered without government authorization and thus do not deserve to be present in the country (see Bosniak 2006; Nevins 2010; Schrag 2011).

Because illegality is the result of immigration restrictions, we must remember that there was a clear racial component to how quotas were assigned in these policies. All the major restrictionist measures implemented through the twentieth century sought to exclude specific racial or national-origin groups from entering the country. Indeed, immigration restriction was used by the federal government to maintain a particular Anglo-Saxon racial makeup of the United States. Immigrants who were unauthorized to enter the United States were defined by their racial and ethnic background. Thus, from the beginning, the American construction of illegality involved obvious concerns about race. Any illegal immigrant who resided in the United States was, by definition of the law, racially undesirable. Even eastern and southern Europeans who were excluded through immigration restriction were deemed to derive from white races inferior to that of the Anglo-Saxon white majority (M. Jacobson 1998; Roediger 2005).

However, the strongly negative reactions we often find encouraged against illegal immigration are not simply rooted in the racial dimension of immigration policy. The term "illegal" is used to denote those engaging in criminal behavior. Ngai (2004) argues that it is through the *implementation* of restrictionist immigration policies that the state cultivates a correspondence between illegal immigration and criminal behavior in general. Once immigration restrictions were outlined, they required surveillance and policing in order to uphold the policy. At first, immigration officers were required to maintain quotas by denying entry to those without a visa. But as the number of migrants who failed to follow quota procedures increased, efforts to capture and deport those migrants also expanded. Patrolling that originally occurred along the border began to spread into the interior of the country as agents began to search for illegal immigrants who had already entered the country. Persistent media portrayals of policing activities that culminate in the apprehension and arrest of illegal immigrants have effectively encoded a clear correspondence between illegal immigrants and other criminals, such as thieves and murderers, within the minds of Americans (Abrajano and Singh 2009). As a result, illegal immigrants are likely to induce the same negative affect that most Americans feel toward violent criminals (see Ono and Sloop 2002).

Rising public concern about illegal immigration also corresponds with changing American norms about race. Early restrictionist policies were explicitly racialized through the national-origin quotas. However, immigration and citizenship law changed in the wake of civil rights policies that sought to combat racial inequities. Changes made in the 1965 Immigration and Nationality Act shifted restriction from being based on national origin to a preference system based on merit and the immigrant's perceived economic contribution. These changes in immigration law aligned with the new race-neutral message American officials sought to promote. Today, immigrants cannot be excluded on the basis of their race but because they do not meet the educational and economic requirements set by law. Legal immigrants thus are deemed as deserving because they hold what Americans have deemed desirable characteristics, but illegal immigrants are not because they have been denied a legal visa. Thus illegal immigration provides a socially acceptable and race-neutral context in which to discuss immigration restrictions.

It should also be noted that while policy makers attempted to make the 1965 norms racially neutral, contemporary immigration policy continues to create racial biases in migration patterns. Those who are deemed meritorious because they meet the educational and economic requirements are eligible for a legal visa. Most commonly, these migrants who are eligible for a legal visa reside in developed nations such as Canada as well as areas in Europe and Asia (Department of Homeland Security 2011; see also Junn 2007). Those who do not meet the high socioeconomic status requirements for legal entry must turn to other strategies in order to enter the United States. Today's immigration law, in conjunction with existing American economic demands, has created a growing illegal Latino (or more specifically Mexican) labor class in the country. The Department of Homeland Security estimates that most unauthorized migrants today arrive from Mexico (Hoefer, Rytina, and Baker 2012). As a result, many would argue that in the contemporary era, illegal immigration is publicly perceived to be Latino. Today, research has demonstrated that the concepts "Latino," "illegal," and "criminal" are strongly interconnected in the American mind (Perez 2010).

EXPECTED RACIAL-GROUP DIFFERENCES ON RESTRICTIVENESS TOWARD ILLEGAL IMMIGRATION

Relatively little systematic research has been conducted on the legal-illegal distinction in the context of contemporary American public opinion. However, public opinion surveys that do include questions on the difference between illegal and legal immigration demonstrate overwhelming rejection of illegal immigration. Figure 2.3.1 compares trends we collected for three versions of the question on decreasing immigration: attitudes about legal immigration, attitudes about illegal immigration, and the standard wording that asks about overall immigration (in which the question makes no distinction between legal and illegal immigration).[6] This figure shows that preference for decreased illegal immigration is the strongest among preferences for decrease legal, illegal, or legally unspecified immigration. Attitudes about overall and legal immigration demonstrate similar trends, with national support for decreasing overall immigration hovering around 50% since 2000. National trends, however, mask any diversity found within the general population.

We expect that the normative distinctions between legal and illegal immigration will be more important to whites than racial minority groups. The creation of what we know now as "illegal" immigration is the result of restrictive immigration policies that originally sought to exclude those perceived as racially undesirable from entering the United States. Illegal status has historically been applied to groups considered nonwhite (Ngai 2005). More important, the link between illegal immigration and criminality has effectively framed illegal immigration as a violation of cherished American norms of respect for institutions and fairness. As discussed above, those ranked at the top of the racial hierarchy are those who benefit the most from established laws and norms. Therefore, whites have the strongest desire to uphold those norms. The distinction between illegal and legal immigration will not only matter most to whites, but we expect whites to be the group that responds most negatively to illegal immigration.

We anticipate that the distinction between legal and illegal immigration will matter less to racial minority groups. The illegality frame, which implies a violation of norms, will not resonate as strongly among groups who recognize that many American laws and values do not equally apply to them. We argue that if a racial minority holds restrictive attitudes toward immigration, their level of restrictiveness is not influenced by the distinction between legal and illegal immigration. Rather, for racial minorities, restrictive

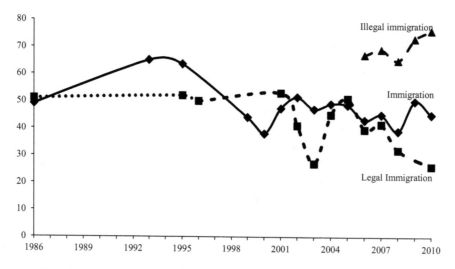

FIGURE 2.3.1 Proportion supporting decrease immigration by type of immigrants, 1986–2010. *Source*: Gallup iPOLL database.

immigration attitudes are generally applied to all types of immigrants. However, given our theory that those minority groups ranked at relatively higher levels on the hierarchy hold stronger desires to uphold the status quo than those groups ranked at the bottom, we expect that illegal-immigration frames will also have varying effects across minority groups. Asian Americans, who are ranked toward the top of the hierarchy, will be more likely influenced by a legal-illegal distinction, since they are more likely to uphold the status quo. In contrast, blacks, who have a historical memory of racially biased laws, are least likely to see a difference between legal and illegal immigration.

Finally, we must take into account the fact that modern frames of illegal immigration have been used primarily to attack Latino immigration. The association between "Latino" and "illegal" may be obvious enough that frames that emphasize illegal immigration likely appear to Latinos as an attack on their racial group. The mechanism that explains Latino response to illegal immigration will be distinct from that which explains responses of other racial groups. Following White's (2007) hypothesis on racial appeals, those appeals that activate an in-group identity will mobilize positive attitudes toward the message. Therefore we expect that illegal-immigration frames may activate Latino identity and that Latinos are likely to respond more positively to illegal immigration than other groups.

EXAMINING ATTITUDES TOWARD LEGAL AND ILLEGAL IMMIGRATION

In this data analysis, we take the first step toward examining the effect of the illegality frame on public opinion about immigration by examining survey items from the 2006 Pew Immigration Survey (Kohut et al. 2006).[7] This survey included a large battery of questions regarding illegal immigration as well as questions about immigration in general. This survey included a nationally representative sample with oversamples of black and Latino respondents. Unfortunately, the sample size of Asian American respondents ($n = 30$) was too small for us to assess here. But, to our knowledge, this 2006 Pew study represents the only publicly available survey that offers systematic analysis of attitudes on illegal immigrant among nonwhite respondents.

The 2006 Pew study offers the opportunity to assess attitudes toward illegal immigrant restriction as well as support for various policy proposals involving illegal immigration.

Because we are examining responses to survey questions on illegal immigration, we cannot identify a direct causal relationship between communication strategies and immigration attitudes in this study. Rather, since our data for this study is a cross-sectional public opinion poll, our analysis can only capture the respondents' immediate or "top of the head" response to illegal immigration. Given the range of survey items available in the 2006 Pew study, we can compare support for relatively lenient policies toward illegal immigrants, such as social welfare provisions, and support for more punitive policies, such as denying birthright citizenship to children of illegal immigrants, in order to compare the degree of restrictiveness toward illegal immigration preferred by different racial groups. Assessing survey responses to illegal immigration in this manner provides us with the baseline attitudes held by the public before manipulation by political communications. More extensive analyses using alternative strategies such as embedded experiments will be required in order to assess how restrictive attitudes might change in response to political communication strategies.[8]

ATTITUDES ABOUT ILLEGAL IMMIGRATION

Respondents in the Pew study were first asked to think about illegal immigration when they were asked by interviewers to compare the problems associated with legal and illegal immigration. When asked what type of immigrants are a bigger problem for the United States, legal or illegal, few respondents believed legal immigration to be the bigger problem. The majority of all respondents believed that illegal immigration was the bigger problem. This is consistent with the growing national attention to the legal-illegal divide that has occurred over the last few decades. The data here confirm that the persistent political frames that emphasize the legal-illegal distinction in immigration have been embraced by the American public. Yet, when comparing responses to this question across racial groups, we do find group differences, as shown in figure 2.3.2.[9] Whites

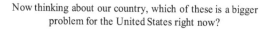

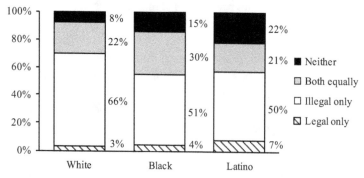

FIGURE 2.3.2 Distribution of responses on type of immigration as bigger problem by race. *Source*: Pew Immigration Survey.

were overwhelmingly (66%) concerned about illegal immigrants, whereas approximately half of black and Latino adults were most concerned with illegal immigration. A larger share of black respondents than white respondents perceived both legal and illegal immigration to be a problem, suggesting that the legal-illegal distinction may not resonate as strongly among blacks as it does for other groups. Latinos represent the group with the largest share of respondents who perceive neither legal nor illegal immigration to be a problem.

It is plausible that the group-level differences in responses to this question may be the result of some biases in the sample population. Racial-group differences on this survey item may not be attributed to race but rather to some other variation between groups, such as educational level. To determine whether attitudes on this illegal-immigration question do, in fact, vary by race and not some other individual characteristic, we conducted multivariate analyses.[10] We found that, even when demographics such as age, education, gender and the respondent's political ideology are controlled for, there were significant differences by race.[11] Both blacks and Latinos are more likely than whites to perceive neither legal nor illegal immigration to be a problem. Blacks were also more likely than whites to believe both legal and illegal immigration are problems. Thus blacks are less likely than whites to emphasize a distinction between legal and illegal immigration. Latinos are also more likely than whites to perceive neither legal nor illegal immigration to be a problem.

However, we find no significant differences between blacks and Latinos in response to this question.

To further investigate this finding, we compare racial-group response to various policy proposals addressing perceived problems related to illegal immigration. The list of policy proposals asked about by Pew is not exhaustive. The policies Pew does ask about, however, represent a realistic sample of those policies most commonly discussed by political leaders over the last few years. Our goal is not to assess perspectives about every dimension of illegal-immigration policy but rather to compare the degree of restrictiveness or willingness to support more punitive measures across racial groups. Table 2.3.1 presents the questions about illegal-immigration policies asked by Pew. In general, most policy proposals involving illegal immigrants involve the removal of rights from those immigrants. However, we can also recognize that some are more retributive than others. Some policy proposals involve wrongdoing by nonimmigrants, such as employer sanctions. Others present extremely restrictive measures such as the denial of birthright citizenship to children of undocumented immigrants.

Responses to illegal-immigration policies are quite varied. While some policy proposals result in clear differences across all three racial groups, others do not. There do, however, appear to be clear differences in opinion between Latinos and the other two racial groups. For example, only 20% of white adults support providing social services to immigrants, and nearly half (46%) support changing the Constitution to deny citizenship status to children of illegal immigrants. By contrast, 64% of Latino adults support providing social services, and only 23% support changing the Constitution. Interestingly, when it comes to providing rights and social services, Blacks attitudes fall squarely in the middle between whites and Latinos. When it comes to verifying legal status, all three groups overwhelmingly support identification policies such as identification cards and eligible-worker databases. Whites and blacks also report similar opinions on the best method to reduce illegal immigrants: slightly over half of both white and black adults support employer sanctions, while Latinos appear to be split over the viability of the proposed options.

Because there were so many policies covered in the 2006 Pew study, we created an index variable that added together responses to the policy proposals presented in table 2.3.1.[12] For this index, we counted the total number of restrictive responses, or those that were directly aimed at restricting behavior of illegal immigrants. Those who were strongly opposed to illegal immigration are those more likely to take the restrictive position on more of these policies. Moreover, since the policies included in the survey represent a range of disciplinary measures, those with higher scores on the index variable reflect those who would

be more likely to support more punitive actions toward illegal immigrants.

Since we seek to identify and compare the degree of restrictiveness against illegal immigrants across racial groups, we examine the distribution of responses on the illegal-immigration policy index. A comparison of the distributions for each of the three racial groups is displayed in figure 2.3.3. We find that the distributions of both white and black respondents are similar across the index. These two groups' responses were skewed toward the more restrictive end of the index. However, larger shares of whites hold extremely restrictive attitudes toward illegal immigrants (score of 4 or 5 on a scale of 5) than blacks. In contrast, Latino responses were more concentrated at the lower end of the index, or the more

TABLE 2.3.1 Distribution of Attitudes on Policies Addressing Illegal Immigration

	% Favor		
	White	**Black**	**Latino**
Should illegal immigrants be required to go home, or should they be granted some kind of legal status that allows them to stay here?			
Required to go home	59	47	19
Allowed to stay	33	47	77
Would you favor or oppose creating a new government database of everyone eligible to work—both American citizens and legal immigrants—and requiring employers to check that database before hiring someone for ANY kind of work?	66	72	61
Would you favor or oppose requiring everyone seeking a new job to have a new kind of driver's license or Social Security card that proves they are US citizens or are in the country legally?	79	78	61
Should illegal immigrants who are in the US be eligible for social services provided by state and local governments?	20	43	64
Should the children of illegal immigrants who are in the US be permitted to attend public schools, or don't you think so?	67	79	93
Which of the following actions do you think would be MOST effective in reducing the number of illegal immigrants who come to the US across the Mexican border			
Increasing number of border patrol agents	33	32	34
Building more fences on the border	9	7	12
Increasing penalties on employers who hire illegal immigrants	52	51	28
Would you favor changing the Constitution so that the parents must be legal residents of the US in order for their newborn child to be a citizen, or should the Constitution be left as it is?	46	36	23

Source: Pew Immigration Survey

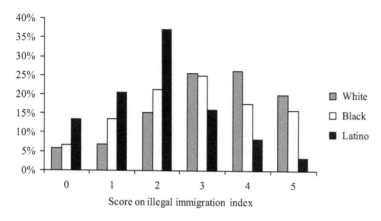

FIGURE 2.3.3 Distribution of responses on illegal immigration policy index by race. *Source*: Pew Immigration Survey.

inclusive position. By calculating the mean scores on our illegal-immigration index, we find that, consistent with our hypothesis, whites' average score is the highest of all groups: 3.20 on a scale of 0 to 5 (standard deviation = 1.40). Latinos' average score is the lowest of the three groups: 1.95 (standard deviation = 1.26). Blacks' average score falls in the middle of the two groups: 2.81 (standard deviation = 1.46).

To again determine if the differences in these means are attributable directly to race and not to another factor such as education or ideology, we turned to multivariate analysis. We used ordinary least squares regression using our illegal-immigration index as the dependent variable and included race, age, education, income, gender, age, foreign-born status, and political ideology as independent variables.[13] We found that when these factors are taken into consideration, both blacks and Latinos report significantly lower scores on our illegal-immigration index than whites. In other words, whites are more likely to support restrictive and punitive measures against illegal immigrants than both blacks and Latinos. Furthermore, we found that Latinos also score significantly lower on the index than blacks. Our multivariate analysis does verify that even when we assume all else is equal, Latinos demonstrate the most inclusive attitudes toward illegal immigrants of the three racial groups studied here.

The data analysis presented here supports our expectation that the racial hierarchy moderates individual responses to illegal immigration. We find that the legal-illegal distinction is most likely to matter among white respondents. We also find that, while many blacks do see a problem with illegal immigration, blacks are more likely than whites to see no difference between legal and illegal immigration. This provides preliminary support for our claim that illegal-immigration frames, which encourage the belief that immigrants violate cherished norms, are less likely to resonate among blacks. Finally, the evidence does support the idea that illegal-immigration frames mobilize Latino in-group identity. Latinos as a group support the most inclusive policies toward illegal immigration. Latinos' positive responses to suggest that Latinos have positive views on those who are part of their racial group. But since this analysis is exploratory, a more detailed examination is needed in order to fully test this assertion.

Priming: The "Face" of Immigration

One issue dimension that has been used to engage the American public is race. Issues related to race have historically mobilized voting blocs to participate in politics in order to protect their interests. As we noted above, the racial-appeals hypothesis suggests that political elites can manipulate public opinion by linking social deviance of racial minorities to a particular issue or policy (Mendelberg 2001). By priming the audience to think about the racial background of those affected by the proposed policy, elites seek to activate racist thinking or resentment. Research has found that when resentment is activated, whites are more likely to support proposed punitive policy solutions to a problem (Entman and Rojecki 2000. Hurwitz and Peffley 2005; Valentino et al. 2002). As a result, racial appeals are assumed to have robust and predictable effects in mobilizing negative responses from white voters.

The racial-appeals hypothesis has been applied recently to issues of immigration policy. Brader, Valentino, and Suhay's (2008) extensive test of the racial-appeals hypothesis on immigration attitudes confirmed that white respondents voice stronger opposition to immigration when primed to think about Latino immigrants than when they are primed to think about European immigrants.

Racial-appeals strategies are assumed to be powerful because they are believed to activate automatic stereotyping (Devine 1989). In controlled environments where individuals have enough time to process information, they can often control how they apply negative stereotypes and prejudice. However, since racial stereotypes are deeply embedded in society, people will be prone to apply those stereotypes in relevant situations. Racial appeals present negative stereotypes in such convincing ways that these messages encourage unintended reliance on those stereotypes. However, as we demonstrate in chapter 3, the tendency to apply stereotypes is determined by one's position in the racial hierarchy. Those at the top of the hierarchy are likely to apply only positive traits to one's own in-group and primarily negative traits to out-groups. In contrast, those groups at the bottom of the hierarchy are less likely to engage in negative stereotyping of out-groups. Thus, it is questionable whether priming racial minorities to think about nonwhite groups will activate automatic negative stereotyping. As White (2007) notes, if the recipient matches the race of the target in a racial appeal, then those appeals can have the opposite effect. Racial appeals may prime positive in-group identities if the appeal primes the respondent to think of his or her own racial group.

EXPECTED DIFFERENCES IN PRIMING EFFECTS ACROSS RACIAL GROUPS

We argue that racial appeals can have predictable effects on activating negative thinking about race, but only for those in the targeted audience for which that appeal was designed. The racial-appeals hypothesis requires more explicit recognition of the match between the racial group used in the appeal and the race of the audience. Priming the audience to think about a nonwhite group will likely generate negative racial thinking only among whites. The same appeal should be expected to have systematically different effects on racial minorities.

In the context of immigration, we expect that priming the audience to think about nonwhite groups entering the United States will encourage more restrictive views among whites. The finding of Brader, Valentino, and Suhay (2008) will thus be replicable in other studies. Based on theories connecting power and stereotyping [...] (Fiske 1993), we argue that because whites rank at the top of the hierarchy, they are prone to negatively stereotype lower-ranked racial groups. Whites' stereotyping is directly attributed to their structural position at the top of the hierarchy: as the most powerful and high-status group, they can be more reliant on schematic thinking, as there are few incentives to pay detailed attention to lower-status groups. Whites' ranking at the top of the hierarchy also means that they are most invested in maintaining the racial hierarchy. Therefore, whites are most likely to attribute positive stereotypes to the higher-ranked groups and negative stereotypes to lower-ranked groups.

For the group ranked at the bottom of the hierarchy, blacks, racial primes that highlight the nonwhite background of immigrants will not automatically mobilize restrictive immigration attitudes. Consistent with our discussion of stereotyping, blacks are less likely to apply negative traits to out-groups. Thus, priming blacks to think about nonwhite groups will not necessarily trigger negative stereotyping. Because blacks are ranked at the bottom of the hierarchy, they are encouraged to pay greater attention to detail rather than be reliant on schematic thinking. For blacks, it is unlikely that race alone will mobilize restrictive attitudes. More information about those immigrant groups will be needed in order to generate perceptions of group threat among blacks.

The effect of racial priming on Asian American and Latino attitudes is expected to correspond to each group's relative position on the racial hierarchy. Since Asian Americans are ranked closer to the top of the hierarchy, racial priming will have an effect on Asian American attitudes on immigration as similar to its effect on white attitudes. We anticipate that because the racial hierarchy gives advantage to Asian Americans, they will seek to uphold that hierarchy. We can expect that, like whites, Asian Americans will attribute positive stereotypes to higher-ranked groups and negative stereotypes to lower-ranked groups. In contrast, since Latinos rank closer to the bottom of the hierarchy, alongside blacks, we expect racial primes to have effects on Latino attitudes on immigration similar to its effect on black attitudes. However, because Asian Americans and Latinos share the same racial categories as the majority of today's new immigrants, it is also likely that racial priming in the context of immigration will highlight in-group racial identities for Asian Americans and Latinos. Therefore, we anticipate Asian and Latino respondents to report more positive attitudes toward immigrants when they are primed to think of their own group.

EXPERIMENTAL DESIGN: TESTING PRIMING EFFECTS

To examine how priming the race of the immigrant may influence public opinion, we turn to experimental design. One of the difficulties of studying how the race of the immigrant might affect attitudes is that researchers are uncertain whom a respondent is picturing when asked a question about "immigrants." Experimental design, which controls the information offered to the respondent, provides us with the most effective way of determining the direct connection between the specific race of the immigrant and a respondent's evaluation of immigration. In our 2006 Faces of Immigration Survey, we included an embedded survey experiment that allowed us to determine how the race of the immigrant may influence attitudes. In these experiments our goal was simply to prime respondents to think about those immigrants as a particular racial group before responding to questions about immigration and immigration policy.

For this experiment, we employed a split-third design in which respondents were randomly assigned to receive one of three conditions. As part of the treatment, all respondents were shown the caption: "The United States is experiencing a significant wave of immigration, and more than 10 million people from other countries have entered the United States since 1996." Those respondents assigned to the Asian-immigrant treatment group were shown a photograph of Asians along with the caption. Those assigned to the Latino-immigrant treatment group were shown a picture of Latinos along with the caption. Those assigned to the control group were provided only the caption, without a photograph.[14] Our strategy was to provide a cue to race and ethnicity by presenting respondents with photographs of immigrants rather than explicitly asking about a particular immigrant ethnic group.[15] We selected photographs designed to prime the respondent to think about a specific racial or ethnic group but did not communicate a specific negative or positive stereotype about that group. The immigrants portrayed in our experimental treatment were not pictured as particularly menacing or aggressive; rather, the photographs depict immigrant families standing in public places. These photos represent the type of immigrants that native-born Americans would encounter in their daily lives.[16] Our goal was to vary only the race of the immigrants, not to encourage respondents to think of particular stereotypes. We selected these manipulations because our goal was not to activate automatic negative affect about immigrants but to see how attitudes might shift if respondents were primed to think of particular groups entering the country.[17]

After viewing the treatment, respondents were then asked to share their attitudes on immigration policy. Our dependent variable is the standard question asked in a public opinion survey, which asks respondents whether they felt the number of immigrants to the United States should be increased, reduced, or kept the same. We coded this measure on a range of 0 to 1, with the preference for reducing immigration "a lot" representing the highest value. To analyze the effect of the treatment, we calculated the average responses for each treatment group on our three dependent variables. Since respondents were randomly assigned to a treatment group, we can identify priming effects by comparing how the mean responses to the question differ across treatment groups and across racial groups.

With this design, we can test multiple comparisons. First, we can compare responses across treatment groups to examine how changing the face of the immigrant causes shifts in opinion on immigration. The first comparison is between those respondents who received the Asian treatment and those who received the Latino treatment. We chose an Asian and a Latino prime in an attempt to examine how the contemporary racial hierarchy influences evaluation of immigrants.

Since Asians are ranked above Latinos on the racial hierarchy, the difference in responses to the two treatment groups will reveal dependence on hierarchical thinking. Second, our data offer us the opportunity to examine how racial priming may have different effects across racial groups. This allows us to test, for example, whether white respondents exposed to the Latino prime report more restrictive attitudes than black respondents exposed to the same prime.

Finally, this design also allows us to identify the racial "face" of the immigrant that respondents picture when asked to provide their assessments about immigration more broadly. Respondents assigned to the control group were not provided a picture of immigrants and were simply asked to provide their attitudes about immigration. Answers provided by the control group thus likely mirror the attitudes found in other public opinion surveys (who are not primed by researchers to think about a particular racial group). Therefore, by comparing the responses of the treatment groups to the responses of the control group, we can make inferences about the assumptions respondents make about the race of the immigrant. If responses from one treatment are similar to those from the control group, then we can reason that the treatment did not cause respondents to alter their assumptions about the immigrants in question. A treatment that provides the expected image of immigrants will not force respondents to make new considerations that they would not have made otherwise. For example, if there are no significant differences between the responses of those who received the Asian treatment group and those who received the control group, then we can surmise that respondents are likely assuming that the immigrants are Asian when they answer questions about immigration. More likely, given the political emphasis on Latino immigration today, responses from the Latino treatment group will be similar to those in the control group.

COMPARING PRIMING EFFECTS ACROSS RACIAL GROUPS

Table 2.3.2 provides the mean responses from each treatment group to question about increasing, decreasing, or keeping immigration the same. In order to understand the effect of the treatment correctly, we first identify a baseline for immigration attitudes. To do this, we point to responses among those in the control group because these respondents were unprimed to think about a particular racial group. Focusing first on the results for whites, we find that whites in the control group strongly support decrease in immigration (mean of 0.8 on a scale of 0 to 1). Comparing means across treatment groups, we find that whites who received the Asian treatment report less restrictive attitudes toward immigration. However, mean responses among whites who received the Latino treatment are no different from those in the control group. There are also no significant differences in means between whites in the Asian treatment and those in the Latino treatment.

Like whites, black respondents in the control group strongly support a decrease in immigration

TABLE 2.3.2 **Mean Responses to Immigration Measures by Race and Treatment Group**

Race of respondent	Mean for Asian treatment (SD)	Mean for Latino treatment (SD)	Mean for control group (SD)	Diff. in means btwn Asian and control group	Diff. in means btwn Latino and control group	Diff. in means btwn Asian and Latino treatment
Whites	.73 (.24)	.76 (.24)	.8 (.24)	−.07**	−.03	−.03
Blacks	.71 (.24)	.70 (.22)	.76 (.22)	−.05*	−.06*	.01
Asians	.58 (.24)	.54 (.25)	.54 (.27)	.04	.01	.03
Latinos	.68 (.25)	.68 (.26)	.66 (.27)	.02	.02	.003

Source: 2006 Faces of Immigration Survey
*$p < 0.10$
**$p < 0.05$

(mean of. 76 on a scale of 0 to 1). However, the racial primes had different results for black attitudes on immigration than we found for whites. Blacks who were primed to think about either Asians or Latinos reported less restrictive attitudes on the increase, decrease, or keep immigration the same measure. These experimental results for blacks suggest that racial primes may not have the anticipated effect on black attitudes on immigration. In fact, the results suggest that racial priming can encourage positive attitudes toward immigrants.

While we find priming effects for both white and black respondents, we find almost no priming effects for Asian American and Latino respondents.[18] Asian American respondents in the control group hold relatively inclusive attitudes toward immigration. Asian Americans' mean score on the increase, decrease, or keep immigration the same measure is near the median value, telling us that Asians are more likely to prefer immigration to stay the same rather than be decreased. Latino respondents in the control group also report relatively inclusive views toward immigrants. Latino respondents report slightly more restrictive responses to immigration (mean = 0.66) than Asian Americans (mean = 0.54), but Latinos' average score is still lower than that reported by both whites and blacks in the control group.[19] Interestingly, we find that the experimental treatments have no effect on altering immigration attitudes among either Asian American or Latino respondents. While we anticipated that Asian American and Latino respondents would respond more positively to immigrants of their shared racial group, our experiment shows that this is not the case. Our results suggest that Asian Americans and Latinos hold relatively firm and positive attitudes about immigration and are not influenced by racial priming.

Finally, to test whether racial priming causes higher-ranked racial groups to report more restrictive attitudes than lower-ranked groups, we compare mean differences across racial groups among those who received the same experimental treatment. Focusing first on those respondents who received the Asian immigrant treatment, we find that there are no significant differences between the mean scores of whites and blacks on the question about increasing,

decreasing, or keeping immigration the same. However, whites' mean scores are significantly higher than both Asian Americans' and Latinos'.[20] This means that whites primed to think about Asians report more restrictive attitudes than Asian American and Latino respondents who received the same treatment. Asian American respondents who received the Asian treatment report the most positive attitudes toward immigration of all four groups who received the Asian immigrant treatment. However, we find significant differences between whites and blacks among those respondents who received the Latino treatment. We find that, of those who received the Latino treatment, whites' mean score is the highest of all four groups. In other words, whites primed to think about Latinos report the most restrictive attitudes. Interestingly, among those primed to think about Latinos, Asian American respondents report the most positive attitudes toward immigration.

In sum, our experiment confirms that racial priming has the most predictable effect on white attitude formation. Among whites, we found few differences in attitude between those who were primed to think about Latinos and those assigned to the control. This suggests that when whites are asked about immigration, without any reference to race, they assume that the immigrant is Latino. Thus, once we encourage whites to think about racial groups ranked highly on the racial hierarchy, such as Asian Americans, they are more likely to hold more open views toward immigration. Comparing mean responses across racial groups, we find that racial primes are likely to encourage whites to report more restrictive attitudes than racial minorities. Out of all racial groups, whites reported the most restrictive attitudes toward immigrants when primed to think about Latinos.

In contrast, we found evidence to support our hypothesis that for blacks, racial primes do not necessarily activate ethnocentrism or negative affect. We found that while blacks generally report more restrictive attitudes than Asian Americans or Latinos, their attitudes became more inclusive when they were primed to think about Latinos or Asian immigrants. It appears that instead of triggering negative responses, our racial primes humanized immigrants for black respondents. These results also tell us that for blacks, the ranking of the racial group is less likely to alter responses to immigration. For whites, we found different effects between those who received the Asian treatment and those who received the Latino treatment. But for blacks, both racial primes had the same effect.

Finally, our experiment yielded very few significant results from the Asian American and Latino respondents. Given that the two largest immigrant flows into the United States are from Asia and Latin America, we assumed that Asian and Latino respondents would rely on shared social-group identities when forming opinions. So we anticipated that, unlike whites and blacks, who do not perceive a shared racial identity with today's new immigrants, Asian Americans and Latinos would be more likely to respond positively to images of immigrants who share their racial background. When examining general trends on immigration attitudes, we found that Asians and Latinos indeed hold more positive attitudes toward immigration than whites and blacks. However, we found no indication that racial primes activate positive in-group identity among Asian American or Latino respondents. This may be because of the fact that Asian Americans and Latinos hold generally positive views on immigration, so racial primes do not have an additive effect on their attitudes.

The Racial Prism and Political Communications

Overall, the findings summarized in this chapter tell us that members of different racial groups respond to political communications in different ways. When political elites design an advertisement or write a speech that employs a racial appeal, that appeal will not have the same effect on all audience members unless the audience is racially homogeneous. Members of racial groups hold different assumptions about their social world, which causes each group to respond differently to political stimuli. The findings discussed in this chapter are useful for moving forward in developing more complex theories on political psychology and communications.

Most important, our evidence demonstrates not only that race dictates the starting assumptions individuals hold but also that the racial hierarchy is deeply embedded in the content of those assumptions. The assumption that nonwhite groups activate negative affect assumes that there is a salient racial hierarchy in which whites represent the most desirable group and nonwhites represent the deviant and undesirable groups. Furthermore, cherished norms such as the assumed just nature of American law, merit, and fairness all presume that individuals are treated equally by governing institutions. In reality, many legal and governing institutions have disproportionately disadvantaged many different subpopulations in American society. Those who most desire to uphold the cherished laws and norms are those most protected by those institutions. We thus should expect that messages that directly implicate the racial hierarchy will be interpreted differently by each racial group.

The findings discussed in this chapter have implications not only for the development of academic research on political communications but also about the effectiveness of political ads and messages in American campaigns. These findings provide new insight for candidates running for office in increasingly diversifying districts. Although racial diversity once characterized only a few metropolitan areas, today most areas across the nation are no longer homogenous white districts. Growing minority populations mean that candidates must consider how their communication strategies will work on a diversifying population. Candidates must develop messages that, at minimum, will not explicitly offend these growing voting blocs. Furthermore, new communications technologies and the rise of the twenty-four-hour news cycle also mean that any racial appeal that may have been intended for a limited audience will likely be distributed to a nationwide audience within minutes. Candidates must then combat the counter-mobilization efforts that develop in response to their messages. The most effective strategies for campaigns in a diverse society thus cannot ignore race but rather should directly address the challenges created by the racial hierarchy.

NOTES

1. The Wilson ad can be viewed at http://www.youtube.com/watch?v=ILIzzs2HHgY. The Tancredo ad can be viewed on YouTube at http://www.youtube.com/watch?v=j3ERcvnnsiU.

2. Although framing and priming can strongly influence public opinion, the voting public will not necessarily obey every message presented by political elites. Certain individuals are more strongly swayed by political messages than others. Cognitive sophistication, motivation, and even party identification have been found to moderate the effects of framing and priming (Chong and Druckman 2007).

3. See also García Bedolla and Michelson (2009); Hutchings et al. (2006); Perez (2011); Philpot and White (2010); Ramirez 2005; J. Wong (2005).

4. The American choice to employ the term "illegal" is also clearly seen as a purposeful political strategy when we compare the United States with other European countries. In Europe, these immigrants are framed as the "irregular population" or "without papers" (see Cornelius et al. 2004; Koopmans et al. 2005).

5. The distinction between legal and illegal immigration arguably started with the 1882 Chinese Exclusion Act. However, since this act only targeted one particular immigrant group, a clear distinction between legal and illegal immigration that would be applied to immigrants more generally did not arise until 1924 (see Ngai 2005).

6. Data on support for decreasing immigration were gleaned from multiple surveys documented in the Gallup iPOLL database, accessed August 13, 2012, http://www.ropercenter.uconn.edu/cgi-bin/hsrun.exe/roperweb/pom/pom.htx;start=ipollsearch?TopID=15. The questions were on different surveys and conducted by different survey firms, though all questions were asked of a nationally representative sample of respondents.

7. The survey was collected using computer-assisted telephone interviews conducted between February 8 and March 7, 2006. Respondents had the option of conducting the survey in either English or Spanish. This survey included a nationwide sample of 2,000 adults as well as city samples for Chicago, IL; Las Vegas, NV; Phoenix, AZ; and Raleigh-Durham, NC. We limited the analysis to the nationwide sample only. The sample sizes by racial group were whites ($n = 1,499$), blacks ($n = 176$), and Latinos ($n = 185$). The remainder of the same was controlled for as "other race" in our analyses. The sampling error for the entire sample is ± 3.5 percentage points. For additional information about this survey see http://www.pewhispanic.org/2006/03/30/americas-immigration-quandary/.

8. One way to study framing effects is to compare public opinion on immigration before and after a major political event involving illegal immigrants or immigration policy. Media attention to events such as the Proposition 187 campaign or the passage of SB 1070 in Arizona in 2010 (which authorized racial profiling and automatic searches of those suspected to be illegal immigrants) will mean that voters are provided persistent frames in favor of or opposed to illegal immigration. These events provide scholars a natural experiment to test how American public opinion changes in response to persistent media and political attention to illegal immigration. A report by the Field Poll that tracked Californian opinion on Proposition 187 over the last two months leading up to the election found that support for the initiative the changed most among likely white voters, while Latino support remained unchanged (Field and DiCamillo 1994). This finding supports our hypothesis that illegal immigration frames will most likely influence white attitudes. However, we recognize that more extensive analysis of these data is needed to fully verify this pattern.

9. Results for all analyses of the 2006 Pew data reported here were weighted to reflect the national sample. Sample sizes by racial group were 1,499 whites, 176 blacks, and 185 Latinos.

10. We considered responses to the "bigger problem" question to be nominal in nature. Therefore, we used multinomial logit analysis and used those who felt "illegal immigration" was the biggest problem as our comparison group. In these models, we included race, age, education, income, gender, being foreign born, and political ideology as control variables. To observe differences between whites and racial minorities as well as possible differences across racial minority groups, we ran two different multinomial models: one with whites as the excluded category and one with blacks as the excluded category. Appendix tables E.2 and E.3 detail the results.

11. The hypothesis we test here is whether or not difference in responses to illegal immigration vary systematically by race. We thus seek to show, using the control-variable approach, whether or not race is a key factor explaining attitude differences, even if assuming all else is held equal. Questions seeking to determine why these differences occur should employ comparative relational analysis. However, since we believe the existing assumption is that racial groups respond similarly to illegal immigration, we seek to discount that claim attempting to verify that group differences can be attributed systematically to race.

12. However, we excluded responses to the question "Which of the following actions do you think would be MOST effective in reducing the number of illegal immigrants who come to the U.S. across the Mexican border" because it is unclear which of the three response options (increasing border patrol, building more fences, or employer sanction) is the most restrictive option.

13. Because we needed to determine differences between whites and racial minorities as well as possible differences across racial minority groups, we ran two different regression models: one with whites as the excluded category and one with blacks as the excluded category. [...]

14. The sample sizes for the Asian-immigrant treatment group, the Latino-immigrant treatment group, and the control group were 140, 167, and 126 for whites; 139, 142, and 157 for blacks; 148, 113, and 124 for Asians; and 142, 128, and 140 for Latinos. Appendix A documents the experimental treatments.

15. By doing so, we sought to escape the problem that respondents might be influenced by social desirability concerns. Mendelberg (2001) argues that explicit questions about race cause white respondents to change their answers in order to conform with existing social norms about racial equality. Therefore, it is difficult to measure white racial attitudes using direct and explicit racial messages. Rather, she advocates use of implicit or indirect messages such as images, which more subtly prime race to white respondents.

16. The treatments were taken from the US Census Bureau website (http://www.census.gov/multimedia/www/photos/facts_for_features/), which provides public-domain images of Americans.

17. We recognize that this design is distinctively different from most other designs used to test the racial-appeals hypothesis. Scholars usually choose stimuli that encourage specific negative stereotypes of racial minorities. However, in our design, we were more concerned with external validity, so we explicitly attempted to provide images of immigrants that respondents would likely encounter in their daily lives. We recognize that our stimuli may not capture extreme negative responses to immigrants, but any difference in attitudes can be directly attributed to the racial prime.

18. Because our samples of Asian American and Latino respondents include relatively larger shares of immigrants compared to the white and black samples, we also examined the effect of the treatment across only native-born Asians and Latinos. Although native-born Asians and Latinos held more negative attitudes toward immigrants compared to the full samples, we did not find significant effects from the experimental treatment for any of the three measures. Therefore, we present the results for the full Asian and Latino samples in this discussion.

19. Differences of means significant at $p < 0.01$.

20. Statistically significant results reported in this discussion are significant by at least $p < 0.10$.

REFERENCES

Abrajano, Marisa, and Simran Singh. 2009. "Examining the Link between Issue Attitudes and News Source: The Case of Latinos and Immigration Reform." *Political Behavior* 31 (1): 1–30.

Bosniak, Linda. 2006. *The Citizen and the Alien: Dilemmas of Contemporary Membership*. Princeton, NJ: Princeton University Press.

Brader, Ted, Nicholas Valentino, and Elizabeth Suhay. 2008. "What Triggers Public Opposition to Immigration? Anxiety, Group Cues, and Immigration Threat." *American Journal of Political Science* 52 (4): 959–978.

Burns, Peter, and James Gimpel. 2000. "Economic Insecurity, Prejudicial Stereotypes, and Public Opinion on Immigration Policy." *Political Science Quarterly* 115 (2): 201–225.

Chong, Dennis, and James Druckman. 2007. "Framing Theory." *Annual Review of Political Science* 10:103–126.

Conover, Pamela J. 1984. "The Influence of Group Identification on Political Perception and Evaluation." *Journal of Politics* 46 (3): 760–785.

Cornelius, Wayne, Takeyuki Tsuda, Philip Martin, and James Hollifield. 2004. *Controlling Immigration: A Global Perspective*. 2nd ed. Palo Alto, CA: Stanford University Press.

Department of Homeland Security. 2011. *Yearbook of Immigration Statistics: 2010*. Washington, DC: US Department of Homeland Security, Office of Immigration Statistics.

Devine, Patricia. 1989. "Stereotypes and Prejudice: Their Automatic and Controlled Components." *Journal of Personality and Social Psychology* 56:5–18.

Druckman, James. 2010. "What's It All About? Framing in Political Science." In *Perspectives on Framing*, edited by Gideon Keren, 279–302. New York: Psychology Press.

Druckman, James, Cari Hennessy, Kristi St. Charles, and Jonathan Webber. 2010. "Competing Rhetoric over Time: Frames versus Cues." *Journal of Politics* 72 (1): 136–148.

Druckman, James, and Kjersten Nelson. 2003. "Framing and Deliberation: How Citizens' Conversations Limit Elite Influence." *American Journal of Political Science* 47 (4): 729–745.

Entman, Robert, and Andrew Rojecki. 2000. *The Black Image in the White Mind: Media and Race in America*. Chicago: University of Chicago Press.

Field, Mervin D., and Mark DiCamillo. 1994. "Big Drop in Support for Prop. 187, The Anti-Illegal Immigrant Measure." Field Poll Release no. 1734, Field Institute, San Francisco.

Fiske, Susan. 1993. "Controlling Other People: The Impact of Power on Stereotyping." *American Psychologist* 48 (6): 621–628.

Gamson, William A. 1992. *Talking Politics*. New York: Cambridge University Press.

Gamson, William A., and Andre Modigliani. 1987. "The Changing Culture of Affirmative Action." In *Research in Political Sociology*, vol. 3, edited by Richard D. Braungart, 137–177. Greenwich, CT: JAI.

García Bedolla, Lisa, and Melissa Michelson. 2009. "What Do Voters Need to Know? Testing the Role of Cognitive Information in Asian American Voter Mobilization." *American Politics Research* 37:254–274.

Henry, P. J., and David Sears. 2000. "The Symbolic Racism 2000 Scale." *Political Psychology* 23 (2): 253–283.

Hoefer, Michael, Nancy Rytina, and Bryan Baker. 2012. "Estimates of the Unauthorized Immigrant Population Residing in the United States: January 2011." Washington, DC: Department of Homeland Security, Office of Immigration Statistics.

Hurwitz, Jon, and Mark Peffley. 2005. "Playing the Race Card in the Post–Willie Horton Era: The Impact of Racialized Code Words on Support for Punitive Crime Policy." *Public Opinion Quarterly* 69:99–112.

Hutchings, Vincent, Nicholas Valentino, Tasha Philpot, and Ismail White. 2006. "Racial Cues in Campaign News: The Effects of Candidate Strategies on Group Activation and Political Attentiveness among African Americans." In *Feeling Politics: Emotion in Political Information Processing*, edited by David P. Redlawsk, 165–186. New York: Palgrave Macmillan.

Iyengar, Shanto, and Donald Kinder. 1987. *News That Matters: Television and American Opinion*. Chicago: University of Chicago Press.

Jacobson, Matthew Frye. 1998. *Whiteness of a Different Color: European Immigrants and the Alchemy of Race*. Cambridge, MA: Harvard University Press.

Junn, Jane. 2007. "From Coolie to Model Minority: U.S. Immigration Policy and the Construction of Racial Identity." *Du Bois Review* 4 (2): 355–373.

Kohut, Andrew, Roberto Suro, Scott Keeter, Carroll Doherty, and Gabriel Escobar. 2006. *America's Immigration Quandary: No Consensus on Immigration Problem or Proposed Fixes*. Washington, DC: Pew Research Center for the People and the Press and Pew Hispanic Center. Accessed January 22, 2007. http://pewhispanic.org/files/reports/63.pdf.

Koopmans, Ruud, Paul Statham, Marco Guigni, and Florence Passy. 2005. *Contested Citizenship: Immigration and Cultural Diversity in Europe*. Minneapolis: University of Minnesota Press.

Mendelberg, Tali. 2001. *The Race Card: Campaign Strategy, Implicit Messages, and the Norm of Equality*. Princeton, NJ: Princeton University Press.

Nevins, Joseph. 2010. *Operation Gatekeeper: The Rise of the "Illegal Alien" and the Remaking of the U.S.-Mexico Border*, 2nd ed. New York: Routledge.

Newton, Lina. 2008. *Illegal, Alien, or Immigrant: The Politics of Immigration Reform*. New York: New York University Press.

Ngai, Mae. 2004. *Impossible Subjects: Illegal Aliens and the Making of Modern America*. Princeton, NJ: Princeton University Press.

Nicholson, Stephen. 2005. *Voting the Agenda: Candidates, Elections, and Ballot Propositions*. Princeton, NJ: Princeton University Press.

Ono, Kent, and John Sloop. 2002. *Shifting Borders: Rhetoric, Immigration, and California's Proposition 187*. Philadelphia: Temple University Press.

Pantoja, Adrian, Ricardo Ramirez, and Gary Segura. 2001. "Citizens by Choice, Voters by Necessity: Patterns in Political Mobilization by Naturalized Latinos." *Political Research Quarterly* 54 (4): 729–750.

Perez, Efren. 2010. "Explicit Evidence on the Import of Implicit Attitudes: The IAT and Immigration Policy Judgments." *Political Behavior* 32 (4): 517–545.

———. 2011. "Black Ice? Race and Political Psychology of Implicit Bias." Paper presented at the 2011 Annual Meeting of the Midwest Political Science Association, Chicago.

Philpot, Tasha S., and Ismail White, eds. 2010. *African-American Political Psychology: Identity, Opinion, and Action in the Post–Civil Rights Era*. New York: Palgrave Macmillan.

Ramirez, Ricardo. 2005. "Giving Voice to Latino Voters: A Field Experiment on the Effectiveness of a National Nonpartisan Mobilization Effort." *Annals of the American Academy of Political and Social Science* 601:66–84.

Roediger, David R. 2005. *Working toward Whiteness: How America's Immigrants Became White; The Strange Journey from Ellis Island to the Suburbs*. New York: Basic Books.

Schrag, Peter. 2010. *Not Fit for Our Society: Immigration and Nativism in America*. Berkeley: University of California Press.

Sniderman, Paul M., and Sean Theriault. 2004. "The Structure of Political Argument and the Logic of Issue Framing." In *Studies in Public Opinion: Attitudes, Nonattitudes, Measurement Error, and Change*, edited by Willem Saris and Paul M. Sniderman, 133–165. Princeton, NJ: Princeton University Press.

Valentino, Nicholas. 1999. "Crime News and the Priming of Racial Attitudes during Evaluations of the President." *Public Opinion Quarterly* 63:293–320.

Valentino, Nicholas, Vincent Hutchings, and Ismail White. 2002. "Cues That Matter: How Political Ads Prime Racial Attitudes during Campaigns." *American Political Science Review* 96:75–90.

White, Ismail. 2007. "When Race Matters and When It Doesn't: Racial Group Differences in Response to Racial Cues." *American Political Science Review* 101:339–354.

Wong, Janelle. 2005. "Mobilizing Asian American Voters: A Field Experiment." *Annals of the American Academy of Political and Social Science* 601:102–114.

Zaller, John R. 1992. *The Nature and Origins of Mass Opinion*. New York: Cambridge University Press.